Fly Fishing
North Carolina

A No Nonsense Guide to Top Waters

Anthony Vinson Smith

Eyes on the prize. Deep in the mountains of western North Carolina, Jonathan Williamson focuses on his fly placement in a riffle on the Cataloochee Creek.

NO NONSENSE

Tucson, Arizona

Fly Fishing North Carolina
A No Nonsense Guide to Top Waters
ISBN-13 978-1-892469-21-2
ISBN-13 978-1-61881-242-1 (E-book)
© 2017 Anthony Vinson Smith
Published by:
No Nonsense Fly Fishing Guidebooks
P.O. Box 91858
Tucson, AZ 85752-1858
(520) 547-2462
www.nononsenseguides.com
Printed in U.S.A.

Editors: Howard Fisher, Russ Lumpkin

Maps, Knot illustrations and fly photos:
Pete Chadwell, Dynamic Arts

Photos: Anthony Vinson Smith

Design and Production: Doug Goewey

Front cover: An angler preparing to drift his flies under the verdant growth along the banks of the Cataloochee Creek.

Back cover, top: As the sun begins to set on a perfect evening at Oregon Inlet on the Outer Banks, author Anthony Vinson Smith displays the last catch of the day. *Photo by Betty Brant.*

Back cover, middle: An angler nets a trout on the Cataloochee Creek in the North Carolina mountains.

Back cover, bottom: David Dow casts for false albacore in the volatile waters of Cape Lookout.

The No Nonsense Creed

The best way to go fly fishing is to find out a little something about a water, then just go there. Experimentation, trial-and-error, wrong turns, surprises, self-reliance, and new discoveries, even in familiar waters, are what make the memories. The next best way is to learn enough from a local to save you from going too far wrong. You still find the water on your own, and it still feels as if you were the first to do so.

This is the idea for our unique No Nonsense fly fishing series. Our books reveal little hush-hush information, yet they give all you need to find what will become your own secret places.

Painstakingly pared down, our writing is elegantly simple. Each title offers a local fly fishing expert's candid tour of his or her favorite fly fishing waters. Nothing is oversold or out of proportion. Everything is authentic, especially the discoveries and experiences you get after using our books. In his outstanding book *Jerusalem Creek,* Ted Leeson echoes our idea: "Discovering a new trout stream is a wonderful thing, and even if its whereabouts are common knowledge, to come upon the place yourself for the first time is nonetheless true discovery."

A RIVER'S PRAYER

Beauty your river rear
Reverent to observe
Even need diligence everywhere
Enough have ecological lost trails
So other rivers slow wondrously yonder
Reaching greater reverence

Even needing greater RESPECT
Together reverence exist tonight
Together RIVERS Salvation NECESSARY!!!!!

William L. Hunt, Jr.

Where No Nonsense Guides Come From

No Nonsense guides give you a quick, clear understanding of the essential information needed to fly fish a region's most outstanding waters. The authors are highly experienced and qualified local fly fishers. Maps are tidy versions of the author's sketches. These guides are produced by the fly fishers and their friends at No Nonsense Fly Fishing Guidebooks.

All who produce No Nonsense guides believe in providing top quality products at a reasonable price. We also believe all information should be verified. We never hesitate to go out, fly rod in hand, to verify the facts and figures that appear in the pages of these guides. The staff is committed to this research. It's hard work, but we're glad to do it for you.

Patient and methodical, an angler casts toward quieter water near the boulder-strewn banks of the beautiful Cataloochee Creek.

Table of Contents

Photo by Capt. Matt Wirt.

5

About the Author

Anthony Vinson Smith is a native North Carolinian and avid outdoorsman. He has lived in a variety of states and had the opportunity to explore many different waters. His parents moved him and his young brother from Raleigh to Chicago when Anthony was three. They made their new home on the edge of Lake Michigan, and for a time, the lake was the center of his outdoor world. Like many young lads, Anthony's father taught him how to fish. Also, his maternal grandparents had a rustic cottage on Scandinavian Lake in Minnesota where fishing for pike and walleye was the primary focus. Over the years his family made many return visits to North Carolina—driving through the mountains, camping, vacationing with cousins at many beaches in the Carolinas, and pier fishing for spots with his granddaddy Lois Smith.

The Smiths eventually moved to the outlying suburbs of Chicago, which back in the sixties, was mostly farmland. One day when he was twelve, Anthony was out exploring and happened upon a den of red fox pups, and he was transfixed. The experience led to his enthusiasm for wildlife photography, a passion that remains to this day. The family moved back to the Old North State in 1973, and Anthony finished his last two years of high school in Fayetteville.

Anthony had a great time during the summer of 1974 working as a member of the inaugural Youth Conservation Corps. Based on the old Civilian Conservation Corps, the Y.C.C. in North Carolina was an organized group of 100 selected teenagers in two teams who maintained trails, built footbridges, and cleaned streams in different areas of the state. Anthony remembers working at Pilot Mountain State Park near the Yadkin River: "My nickname was 'Scout.' We lived in military tents and everyone bunked on cots that looked like a scene from the TV series *M.A.S.H.."* That area is now a historic site known as Horne Creek Farm.

Moving "Down East" to Greenville, he attended East Carolina University as an art major with a minor in broadcasting. His first radio job was with a small rock station where he often prepared news, wrote commercial spots, and worked as a disc jockey. During that time, he and his friend Joseph Corso fished black water creeks and caught a lot of bream with ultra-light spinning gear and crickets.

After several years as a rock jock and program director in various radio markets, Anthony switched to public radio. He moved to Boston where he wrote, voiced, and produced numerous features for MonitorRadio, a broadcast Service of the *Christian Science Monitor.* The "Daily Edition" was heard on more than 100 stations across the nation on the American Public Radio Network. At the end of that period in 1989, Anthony chronicled the Bass Masters Classic that took place on the James River in Richmond, Virginia. As a journalist-angler, he fished with North Carolina's own Hank Parker who wound up winning the event.

The Oregon Trail

Anthony spent the nineties in the Great Northwest. His old buddy Joseph Corso had moved to the Portland area and sent enticing reports of the rivers, streams, and incredible trout, salmon, and steelhead fishing. In the wide-open sagebrush spaces of Oregon, Anthony thrived. He immediately learned to fly fish during a three-day float trip on the Deschutes River. There were numerous jaunts to Washington State and Alaska. Once, while boarding a bus in Denali Park with backpack and monopod in hand, an elderly stranger commented to the bearded Anthony, "You remind me of a young John Muir."

Soon he befriended a fellow photographer named Scott Ripley, a former assistant editor with *Trout* magazine. Toting his camera in a dry bag wherever he went, Anthony's photos and stories began to appear in magazines such as *Fly Fish America, Northwest Fishing Holes, Tight Loop* (Japan), *Steelhead Flyfishing Journal, Salmon Trout Steelheader,* and *Washington Wildlife.* Those were halcyon days in the Northwest, but after a decade, Anthony missed his family and the Carolina sunshine.

Anthony moved to Greensboro in 2000 and began working as a freelance photojournalist. By 2002 he was a regular contributor to the *Greensboro News & Record* outdoors page, chronicling his angling adventures and exploring North Carolina's wild places. Other publications featuring his work have included *Our State, Birds & Blooms, NCBoating Lifestyle,* and *Fly Fishing Virginia.* In fact it was a lengthy conversation with Beau Beasley, the author of the *No Nonsense Guide to Fly Fishing Virginia,* that sparked Anthony to undertake *his* new book, *Fly Fishing North Carolina.*

Anthony Vinson Smith believes in Thoreau's words: "We need the tonic of wildness." He also knows that fly fishing in this beautiful place we call North Carolina is one of the best ways to find it.

Foreword

Giving thanks and reverence to our rivers and streams have always been included in my people's and many Nation's prayers. These waters have always and will forever be sacred and holy for they can cleanse, purify, heal and make holy, not only the people, but our Earth Mother as well. They provide an abundance of fish of all kinds for our wonder and food. I know Anthony, my blood brother, has approached each stream and river with the same reverence and respect as my native ancestors. May you do the same as you visit these waters in North Carolina and please help keep them clean and holy.

William L. Hunt, Jr.
Lumbee/Tuscarora

Big Snowbird Creek, Lower Falls.

Tribute

Several years ago, I visited a library in Greensboro and picked up a copy of *Fly Fishing in North Carolina,* written by the late Buck Paysour. His stories and down-home writing style captivated me. After reading the book, I looked him up, gave him a call, and left a rambling but complimentary message. He called me back and, ironically, profiled me in his fishing column for *ESP* magazine, a Greensboro-based weekly. We had never met although we had traveled some of the same fishing and professional paths. When we did finally meet, I greeted him at his front door and shook his big paw of a hand. He instantly struck me as a genuine sort of guy whom I would enjoy fishing with. My point here is that that there have been many other anglers before me who have written about the beauty and bounty of the Old North State—Charles Kuralt is one other example. And long after I'm gone, some colorful character who shares a passion for fly fishing will write about many of the same streams and lakes and beaches mentioned here. I worked on this book for years, and in each chapter, I tried to keep in mind that human element that binds generation to generation. I hope the influence of folks such as Buck Paysour and Charles Kuralt is apparent. For it is fellow North Carolinians such as them as well as the generous guides, biologists, passionate anglers, family, and fishing buddies, who have inspired me to finally put these chapters together.

Dedication

This book is lovingly dedicated to my mom and dad. My mom opened up my world and imagination by introducing me to words and self-expression. She was the first to instill in me, an appreciation for a good story. She encouraged my interest in art by taking me to places such as the Art Institute of Chicago. Dedicated to her church and family, she has always been supportive and continues to demonstrate grace on a daily basis.

My late dad, a veteran and a patriot, from Durham, used to refer to road trips in our old Rambler station wagon as "adventures." He always exuded a passion for the outdoors. Some of my fondest memories are of camping and fishing at Hatteras or Oregon Inlet. He appreciated my enthusiastic nature and always encouraged my creativity. My dad's memory is always present with me in the field or on the stream.

I would also like to give a shout out to my mom's mom. A retired school teacher living in Minneapolis, Minnesota, my grandmother Margaret Thone lived into her second century.

An angler casts for trout on the Watauga River near Boone on a crisp winter day.

Acknowledgments

Tusen takk is Norwegian for "A thousand thanks." So, tusen takk to the following folks: Scott Ripley, my Oregon photojournalist mentor; Joseph Corso, a lifetime friend and fishing buddy; Elizabeth Larson, a great lady and photographer who was often "my second lens;" *Greensboro News & Record* editors Joe Sirera and Charlie Atkinson; Theo Copeland of the Appalachian Angler; Jeff Wilkins, my fly-tying teacher, friend, and superb guide; Mike Perry, for showing me the Roanoke; David Dow, for taking me to Cape Lookout; Brad Ball, for showing me Linville Gorge; The Nat Greene Fly Fishers, Clarence "Rock" Rothrock and his wife, Lorraine, Gary Edwards, and "Uncle Cecil" Chapman; Triangle Fly Fishers, Jim Burchette and Troy Branham; Virginia's Beau Beasley; Keith Calhoun and his red drift boat on the 'Tuck. A salute goes out to the captains: Capt. Dean Lamont, Capt. Rob Modys, Capt. Gary Dubiel, Capt. Matt Wirt, and Capt. Gordon Churchill. I also wish to thank pirate Mark Bell; entomologist Becky Nichols; The National Park Service; North Carolina State's Dave Penrose, Dr. Jules Silverman, and Jean Carter; North Carolina Division of Water Quality's Eric Fleek; Scott Cunningham of On the Fly Guide Service; Asheville TU's Carey Kirk; and Walker Parrott. Cheers to Max Lloyd who let me fish at "Lake Cabernet;" the late Jeanette "J" Clanton for her patience and support. Best fishes to my sister, Tammy Pegram . . . I hear the music. And finally, much gratitude to editor and publisher, Howard Fisher, and his team for their patience and professionalism.

The author hooks a brookie from the bank of the Nantahala. Photo by Elizabeth Larson.

Fly Fishing North Carolina

North Carolina has it all, from the inlets, sounds, beaches and Outer Banks, to the creeks, streams, and hollers of the Blue Ridge Mountains. In between are the countless farm ponds, mighty rivers, man-made reservoirs, swamps, and pocosins that are home to a great variety of fish. The stage is set for the fly-fishing angler. From here in Greensboro, not exactly a fly fishing destination but centrally located, I can venture out in any direction and find a worthy place to cast a fly. In this book, I invite you to join me as I sample many of the most noteworthy fly-fishing waters across this land. This book does not cover *every* stream, lake or river, but each chapter provides a synopsis of a destination that is representative of the best our state has to offer. It is written from my point of view based on research and personal experience. The maps show you where to go and some key access points. The photography is intended to give you a feel for the tenor of the place. The fly pattern section illustrates some of the best national and regional patterns. If you are new to fly fishing or visiting from another place, a novice or an old master, this book can help you. All are welcome.

Guide and friend, Theo Copeland of the Appalachian Angler fly shop, on his home waters near Boone.

State and National Parks

The Old North State is home to great sanctuaries that include the most visited National Park in the United States, The Great Smoky Mountains National Park. Our state parks, including places such as Hammock's Beach and Fort Macon, are strategically located near some of the best waters anywhere. These parks, along with national forests and recreational areas, often provide the most affordable places to pitch a tent or stay in a cabin. They provide an ideal base camp for exploring a multitude of fly-fishing opportunities.

National Wildlife Refuges

One of the reasons that fly fishing became a real passion with me is because of my love for exploring wild places. A North Carolina mountain stream, lake, or a coastal river can take you through some of the most rugged back country or reveal the most breathtaking vistas. Our wildlife refuges have preserved large tracts of the most prolific wildlife habitats where anglers have unique access. Cedar Island and the Roanoke River top the list of my personal favorite National Wildlife Refuges when it comes to fishing. The Roanoke is home to anadromous fish such as alewife, blueback herring, American shad, hickory shad, and striped bass. Cedar Island's waters include periodic oceanic species such as redfish, sea tout, striped bass, and even tarpon.

Tribal Waters

Native Americans have always had a special kinship with this land. The Eastern Band of the Cherokee Nation manages the waters of the Oconaluftee River and Raven Fork. These streams in and around the town of Cherokee, near Great Smoky Mountains National Park, are well stocked with hundreds of thousands of trout each year. Fly fishers do not need a state license, but must have a tribal permit to fish inside the reservation or *Qualla* boundary. There are special catch and release sections that are home to some trophy trout. These streams have produced state records for brown and brook trout.

Property Rights

Always respect the private property adjacent to water you are fishing. If you want to fish a pond or posted water, seek out, and politely ask the land owner for permission. Generally, a stream that is navigable by boat is within the public domain for fishing and wading. The riparian area and stream banks, if posted, are considered legal private property. The North Carolina Wildlife Resources Commission's annual Inland Fishing Regulations Digest (www.ncwildlife.org) clearly outlines boundary lines and rules to follow. Never trespass. Anglers who trespass, litter or show disregard for the environment make it more difficult for future anglers.

A very handsome array of rigged large arbor reels with rods, courtesy of Marty Leeper.

The author fishing a farm pond in his float tube, a holdover from his days in the Northwest.

Guides

If you are new to fly fishing or a seasoned veteran, enlisting the services of a good guide is one of the best ways to learn more about the art of fly fishing. Guides can update you on the latest flies, techniques, gear, and best places to fish. Hiring a guide is also an excellent way to introduce other family members to the sport, taking away the perceived pressure to find fish and just being able to relax and have fun.

Conservation

Every fly fisher with whom I have ever fished has shown respect for the stream environment by not leaving a tangible trace in the field or stream and most have only taken pictures with them when they leave. Fly Fishers International (FFI) is a Montana-based organization that conserves, restores, and educates through fly fishing (see www.flyfishersinternational.org). Their Casting Instructor Certification Program sets the standard for our art form. FFI is an outstanding resource. They also host an annual Fly Fishing Fair and Conclave.

Trout Unlimited (TU) is another leading national conservation organization that is dedicated to protect, reconnect, restore, and sustain our coldwater fisheries (see www.tu.org). TU has chapters all across the state and its members are fly fishers who donate their time for all sorts of volunteer work such as stream restoration projects. Many of the finest people in the state are associated with TU.

Rivercourse is a conservation and educational program sponsored annually by the North Carolina State Council of Trout Unlimited. Their slogan sums it up: "The future of our coldwater conservation lies in our youth." Their weeklong program for teenagers includes exploration of subjects such as geology, entomology, ecology, stream restoration, fly fishing, and fly tying. For more information about N.C.T.U. Rivercourse Youth Camp, see www.rivercourse.org.

Etiquette

"Creeps and idiots cannot conceal themselves for long on a fishing trip." —John Gierach

Fly fishing is a lot like golf when it comes to matters of etiquette. There are just some things you should never do. For example, it is bad form to fish nearby or in the same direction as another angler. If another angler is moving upstream, you should move farther downstream or much farther upstream. You should give another angler a wide berth of space so as not to spook any potential fish in the area. Leave the area as clean or cleaner than it was. Do not trespass. Do not build fires unless it is a survival situation. Simply practicing the golden rule is your best bet.

Catch and Release

"The finest gift you can give to any fisherman is to put a good fish back, and who knows if the fish that you caught isn't someone else's gift to you." —Lee Wulff

Know the fishery. When I caught fin-clipped steelhead in Oregon I knew they were hatchery fish and therefore the idea of keeping one would not be a threat to their species' survival. 95% of the time I do practice catch and release. However, under proper conditions and within legal regulations, I believe that harvesting a few fish for the kitchen or camp table is acceptable.

Theo Copeland releases a fine Watauga rainbow.

Gear

The fly rod is your first consideration. Often a guide or a veteran fly fisher friend can supply a rod if you are just learning the sport. A "combo" fly rod and reel set can save you money. Most of the streams of North Carolina can be fished with a light 3- or 4-weight rod. Larger rivers and bigger fish might require a 5- or 6-weight rod. Largemouth bass require a rod as stout as an 8-weight. Saltwater rods range from 6-weights for speckled trout to 12-weights or more for species such as sharks. A fly shop or outdoor store specialist can match the proper reel to the rod size. Line is the next consideration. Floating lines, intermediate, and sinking lines are the three most basic. Decide what type of fishing you want to do. The following chapters in this book usually mention what kind of line and leader is most appropriate for the type of water and species. Generally, a tapered leader attached to your floating line works for most situations. Guides or fly shops can be very helpful in determining the right combination for your destination. Good wading boots or shoes are important to provide traction and protection. They will help you keep your balance on slippery stream bottoms or in coastal waters that might have razor-sharp shells.

Fly Shops

Fly shops are outstanding resources for gear and localized information on stream conditions. You can find out what's hot, and what's not. Most fly shops can also refer you to the best guides in the area. Materials for fly tying are readily available as well as nice selections of regional flies. These stores are there to support our sport, so let us be sure to support them.

Safety

Safety of course, is of paramount importance. It is best to always fish with a partner if possible. If not, at least let a loved one know of your intentions, where you will be, when, and for how long. Another prudent idea is to sign in at national park trailheads so that park officials can find you if you get lost or break a leg. Wading boots with good soles will help to keep you from losing your balance on slick stream stones. A wading staff can also be helpful. In the mountains or woodlands, I often employ the use of found sticks that have been gnawed by beavers. These natural staffs can then be set aside when you are done with them. If you are wearing chest waders, wear a belt to cinch them. This will help if you take a spill, so that your waders don't fill up with water

Some favorite fly creations by Jeff Wilkins.

Jeff Wilkins is a knowledgeable guide and instructor in the Greensboro area. An amazing fly caster, he has also perfected the art of tying some unique and beautiful flies. Wilkins has been a good and patient friend as well as an inspiration to the author.

as fast. Polarized glasses are mandatory and work well to help you find fish and see where you are going. They can also protect your eyes from a wayward hook. Bring plenty of water and snacks. Always have extra warm layers in the unlikely event of a water landing. In colder weather it is a good idea not to wear cotton. If you get wet, clothing made from material such as nylon, wool, or polypropylene will dry faster and not be as chilling. Pre-pinching the barbs on your hooks is a good idea in case you later get hooked. It is also better for the fish. Always carry a first aid kit, sunscreen, and bug dope.

Let's Go Fish!

I hope you take advantage of the information contained on these pages. The creation of this book took longer than expected but it has been a labor of love. Fly fishing in North Carolina is fun and I hope that this book reflects that. "The quiet sport" is usually very relaxing and one of the best ways to enjoy the natural beauty and bounty of our great state. Perhaps I will see you down the trail.

Fly fishers in clear waters employ a variety of stealth techniques when approaching wary trout.

Flies to Use in North Carolina—Drys and Terrestrials

Adams Parachute

Black Fur Ant

Black Beetle

Jeff's Beetle

Blue Dun

Blue Quill

Blue-Winged Olive

Blue-Winged Olive Parachute

Blue-Winged Olive Cripple

Elk-Hair Caddis

Light Cahill

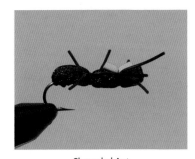

Chernobyl Ant

Coffin Fly

Black Gnat

Griffith's Gnat

Photo: BigYFlyco.com

14

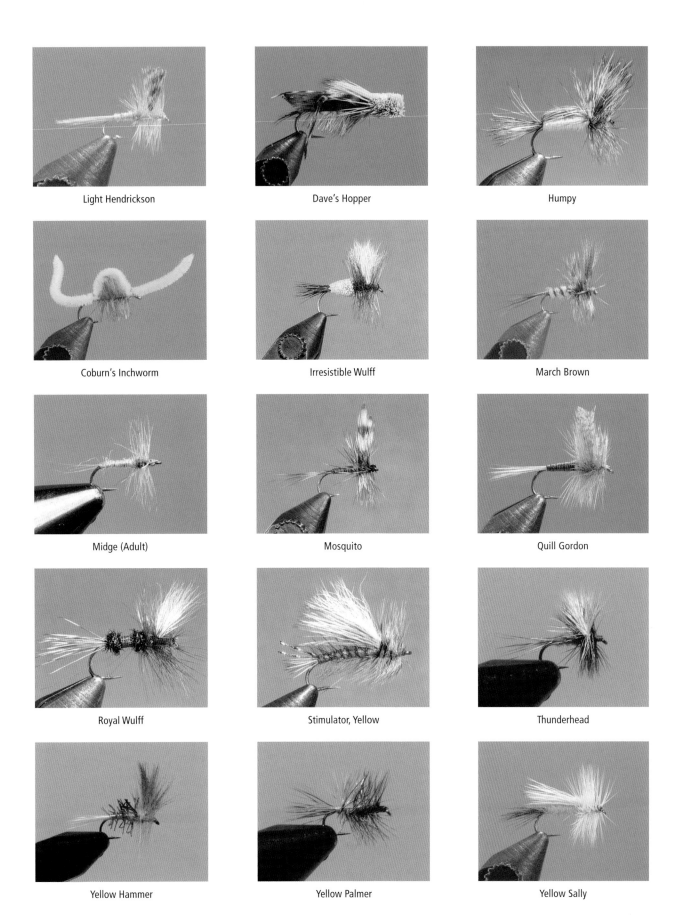

Light Hendrickson

Dave's Hopper

Humpy

Coburn's Inchworm

Irresistible Wulff

March Brown

Midge (Adult)

Mosquito

Quill Gordon

Royal Wulff

Stimulator, Yellow

Thunderhead

Yellow Hammer

Yellow Palmer

Yellow Sally

Nymphs, Streamers, and Wet Flies

Brassie

The Bug

Barr's Copper John

Glo Bug

Gray Ghost

Beadhead Flashback Hare's Ear

Jeff's Rojo Emerger

Jeff's White Maggot

Mickey Finn

Muddler Minnow

Beadhead Pheasant Tail

Flashback Pheasant Tail

Prince Nymph

Prince Nymph (Yellow)

San Juan Worm

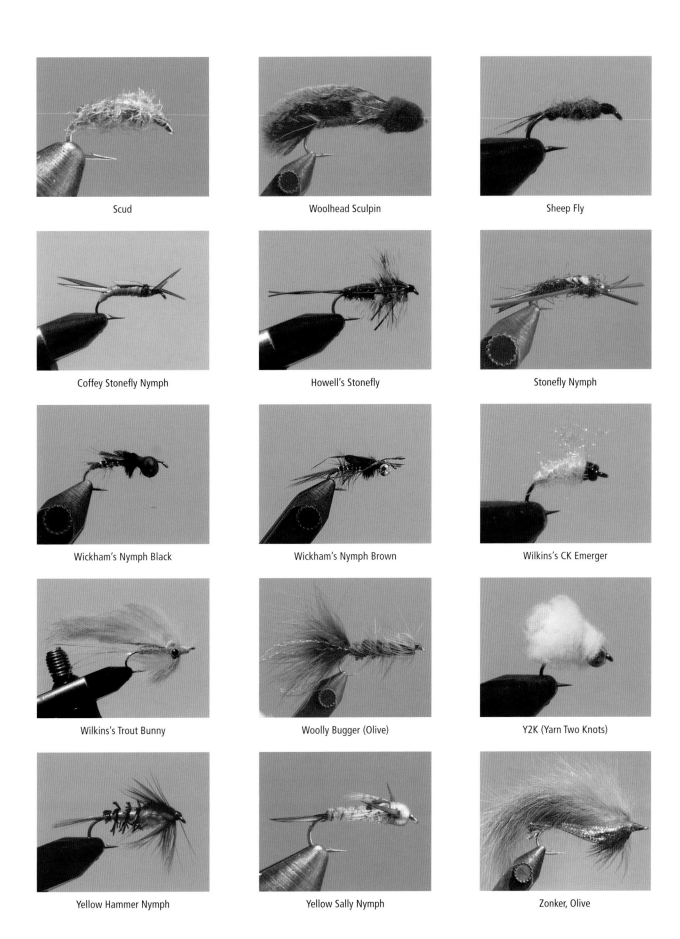

Scud

Woolhead Sculpin

Sheep Fly

Coffey Stonefly Nymph

Howell's Stonefly

Stonefly Nymph

Wickham's Nymph Black

Wickham's Nymph Brown

Wilkins's CK Emerger

Wilkins's Trout Bunny

Woolly Bugger (Olive)

Y2K (Yarn Two Knots)

Yellow Hammer Nymph

Yellow Sally Nymph

Zonker, Olive

Warmwater Flies

Braided Butt Damsel

Chocklett's Disc Slider

Kraft's Clawdad, Brown

Clouser's Crayfish

Clouser's Deep Minnow

Jeff's Deceiver

Howell's Big Nasty

Kevin's Catapiller

Kreelex

McCune's™ Sculpin

Trow's Minnow

Walt's Frog Slider

Whitlock's Crayfish

Whitlock's Deer Hair Popper

Wilkins's Fire Tiger Bass Popper

Saltwater Flies

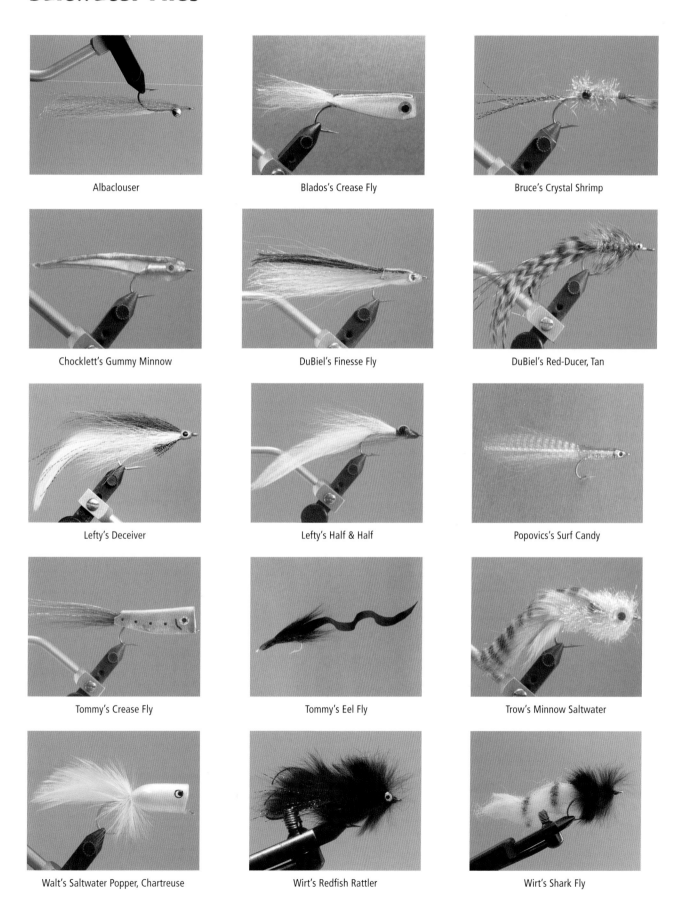

Albaclouser

Blados's Crease Fly

Bruce's Crystal Shrimp

Chocklett's Gummy Minnow

DuBiel's Finesse Fly

DuBiel's Red-Ducer, Tan

Lefty's Deceiver

Lefty's Half & Half

Popovics's Surf Candy

Tommy's Crease Fly

Tommy's Eel Fly

Trow's Minnow Saltwater

Walt's Saltwater Popper, Chartreuse

Wirt's Redfish Rattler

Wirt's Shark Fly

An angler works his way through the delayed-harvest section of the Nantahala.

Top North Carolina Fly Fishing Waters

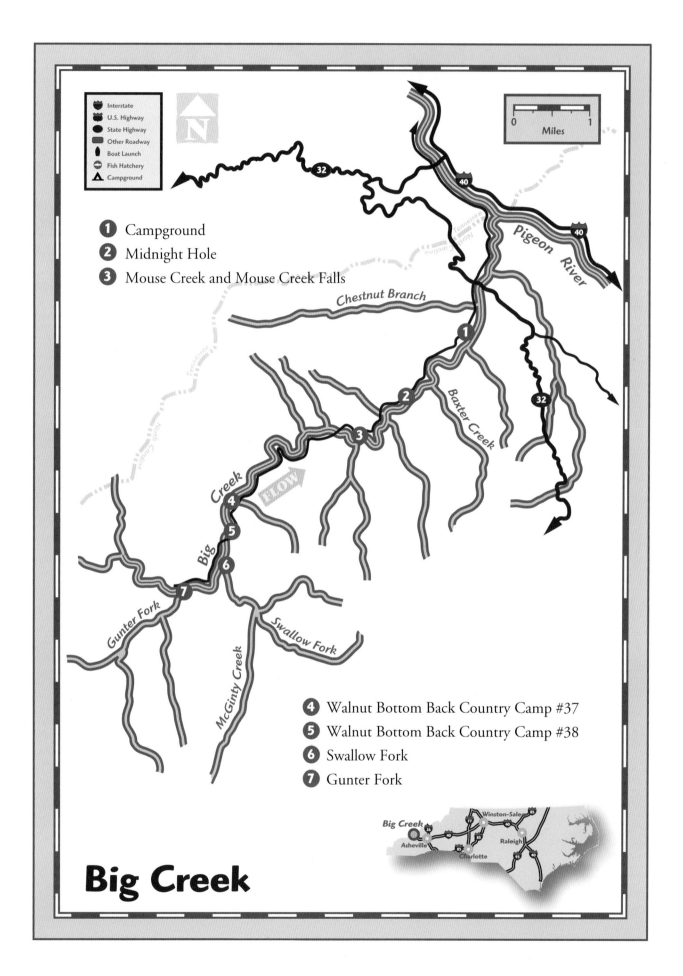

Legend
- Interstate
- U.S. Highway
- State Highway
- Other Roadway
- Boat Launch
- Fish Hatchery
- Campground

1 Campground
2 Midnight Hole
3 Mouse Creek and Mouse Creek Falls

32
40
40
32

Pigeon River

Chestnut Branch

Baxter Creek

Big Creek

FLOW

Gunter Fork

McGinty Creek

Swallow Fork

4 Walnut Bottom Back Country Camp #37
5 Walnut Bottom Back Country Camp #38
6 Swallow Fork
7 Gunter Fork

Big Creek
Asheville
Charlotte
Winston-Salem
Raleigh

Big Creek

Big Creek

Big Creek is a rugged, high-gradient stream with a lot of big boulders, deep pools, and a robust attitude. Located in the northeastern corner of the North Carolina section of Great Smoky Mountains National Park, this stream offers a crystal-clear habitat that makes for spooky fish and difficult stalking.

Big Creek is a medium-size flow that follows an old railroad grade in western Haywood County, but is easy to find because of its proximity to I-40. Big Creek Campground is a walk-in campsite on park grounds that parallel the stream just above its confluence with the Pigeon River and provides a good base camp from which to fish. Most of the trout are not very big but the experience is memorable because the environment is breathtaking. There is, of course the possibility and the persistent rumor of big browns, especially in the lower reaches of the creek. However, a great award awaits the fly fisher who does not mind hiking upstream a few miles or so to find some native brook trout or "specs" as the locals call them, with some rainbows mixed in.

There are some nice pools including Midnight Hole just above the campground and Blue Hole along the main stem three miles up near Mouse Creek Falls. Wading on Big Creek can be difficult,

A fish-eye view of a typical Smoky Mountains rainbow at Big Creek.

Clear water makes for wary trout at Big Creek.

Tim Hamilton nymphs a pool for wild rainbows above the main campsite at Big Creek.

due to the turbulence of the class IV & V whitewater that attracts a few kayakers.

About five miles upstream from the campground parking lot is Walnut Bottoms, a backcountry campground. Careful, though, this is certified bear country, possibly the most likely place in the whole park for an encounter. The brookie habitat upstream in the higher elevations includes Swallow Fork, a major tributary five miles upstream from the main campground. Another mile up from Swallow Fork is Gunter Fork, and each of these tributaries has trail access. Gunter Creek is closed beyond the first trail crossing 1.9 miles up. This section and several other small tributaries are closed to protect the brook trout population and public water supply. These closed streams are posted on site or at park visitor centers.

On a recent spring trip to Big Creek, while camped at the twelve-site tent Big Creek campground, I befriended a fellow fly fisher from Virginia by the name of Tim. He let me follow him around with my camera and document his technique. He preferred to line himself up adjacent to a large boulder and cast downstream while slowly twitching a nymph or streamer behind a rock on the retrieve. This was an effective way to keep the fly in play, allowing it to hover in front of hungry trout. The movement of the nymph pattern or streamer against the softer current resembles an aquatic insect that is striving for the surface or an injured baitfish. Tim was quite successful at landing the feisty rainbows in the typical five- to eight-inch range.

Big Creek is about 50 miles from Asheville, west on I-40 near the Tennessee border at the Waterville exit. Cross the Pigeon River Bridge, turn left on the road past an electric power plant. Travel up the road past the Ranger Station to the campground.

Yellow is a very common color for mayflies in the Blue Ridge Mountains.

Yellow stonefly nymphs are an important part of a trout's diet in the Smoky Mountains.

Types of Fish

Mostly rainbows, with some brook trout upstream and a few browns downstream near Big Creek Campground.

Known Hatches

Black Stonefly, Blue Quill, Blue-Winged Olive, Caddis, Dun Caddis, Early Brown Stone, Giant Black Stone, Giant Brown Stonefly, Green Caddis, Hendricksons, Lead Wing Coachman, Little Black Winter Stone, Little Brown Stone, Little Dark Olive, October Caddis, March Browns, Little Yellow Stoneflies, midges, Sulfurs, Quill Gordon, Inchworms, Tan Caddis, and terrestrials.

Equipment to Use

Rods: 2- to 4-weight, 7 to 8 feet in length.
Reels: Standard mechanical.
Lines: Weight-forward floating, matched to rod.
Leaders: 5x to 7x leaders, 8 to 10 feet in length.
Wading: Chest waders recommended.

Flies to Use

Drys: Adams, sizes 14-20; Black Midge, 18-22; Blue-Winged Olive, 14-20; Elk-Hair Caddis, 14-20; Gray Caddis Pupa, 16-22; Griffith's Gnat, 18-22; Light Cahill, 18-20; Parachute Adams, 14; Royal Wulff, 14-16; Stimulator, 12-18; Sulfur Dun, 16-22; Thunderhead, 12-16.

Nymphs & Streamers: Beadhead Hare's Ear, sizes 14-20; Beadhead Prince Nymph, 14-20; Bullethead Grasshopper, 8-10; Copper John, 14-20; Muddler Minnow, 8-10; Pheasant Tail Nymph, 14-20; Scud, 14-18; Tellico Giant Black Stone Nymph, 6-12; Smoky Mountain Blackbird Softhackle, 14; Thunderhead Nymph, 12-16.

When to Fish

Spring, fall and summer are best.

Season & Limits

Open all year during daylight hours with a 4 fish creel limit. There is a 7-inch limit on rainbows, brook trout, brown trout or smallmouth bass. Only artificial lures or flies may be used with a single hook. A dropper fly rig may be used.

Nearby Fly Fishing

The Cataloochee Valley is about a 35-minute drive from the confluence of Big Creek and the Pigeon River.

Accommodations & Services

Big Creek has a walk-in 12-site tent campground, a picnic area, water, and restrooms. Newport, Tennessee, is the nearest town, just a short drive up I-40.

Rating

Big Creek rates a solid 7.

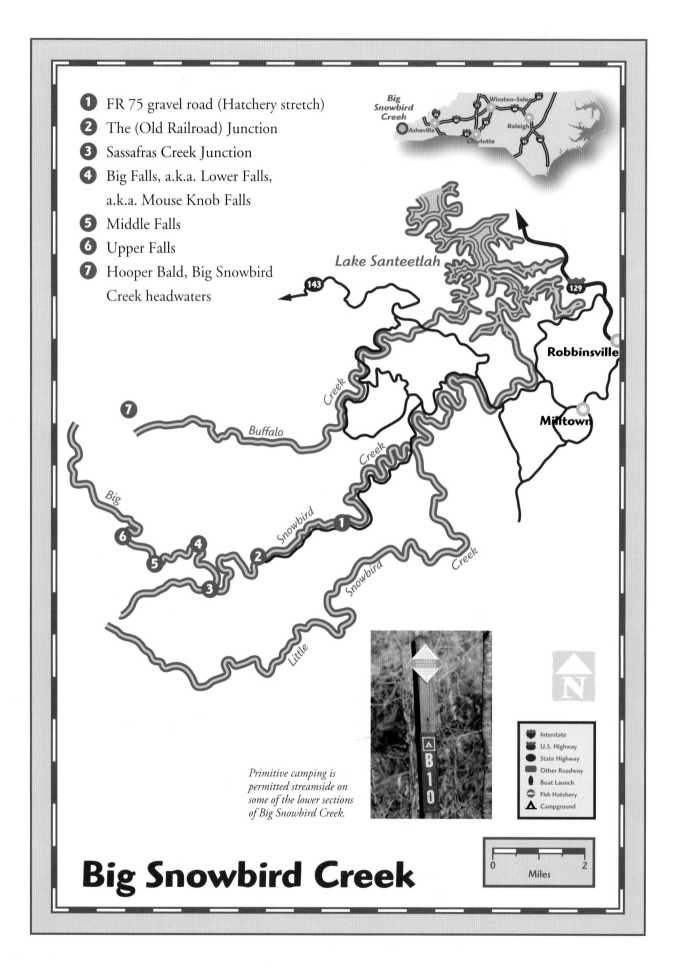

1. FR 75 gravel road (Hatchery stretch)
2. The (Old Railroad) Junction
3. Sassafras Creek Junction
4. Big Falls, a.k.a. Lower Falls, a.k.a. Mouse Knob Falls
5. Middle Falls
6. Upper Falls
7. Hooper Bald, Big Snowbird Creek headwaters

Primitive camping is permitted streamside on some of the lower sections of Big Snowbird Creek.

Interstate
U.S. Highway
State Highway
Other Roadway
Boat Launch
Fish Hatchery
Campground

Miles
0   2

Big Snowbird Creek

Big Snowbird Creek

After an early bout of severe winter weather, we had a warm spell typical of a North Carolina February. For me, that meant a return trek to Big Snowbird Creek before the typical March blizzard. My first visit to Big Snowbird was during an extended camping trip on the Nantahala River with several members of the Nat Greene Fly Fishers Club, based in Greensboro. A couple of us ventured out to Big Snowbird Creek, exploring the area for a few hours. It was an interesting side trip and it left me wanting more.

About thirteen and a half miles southwest of Robbinsville, State Road #1120 (details below) turns into Forest Service road #75. The gravel road dead-ends after six miles at the Big Snowbird Trailhead, a place called "The Junction." The gravel road offers good access to the stream and marked primitive camping areas within the Nantahala National Forest. From "The Junction" parking area, heading upstream, Trail 64 parallels Big Snowbird Creek. This marks the beginning of the walk-in fishing and Wild Trout regulations. This medium-size freestone stream is on the right, and most of the way it is choked with very large rhododendrons. The steep mountainsides are covered with hardwoods. The trail is wet, crisscrossed with various springs and small cascades. The areas of the mountainside that remained in shadows showcased wondrous icicles and ice sculptures. This had been a sacred Cherokee hunting ground, and from the tracks in the traces of snow, the area is still popular hunting grounds for bobcats. Scat proved that indeed, a

Types of Fish
Wild and hatchery-supported rainbows and browns. There are wild brook trout above Lower Falls and "steelhead" in the lower sections that infiltrate from Santeetlah Lake.

Known Hatches
Baetis, Black Caddis, Black Stonefly, Blue Quill, Blue-Winged Olive, Cream Midge, Gray Caddis, Gray Fox, Hendrickson, Isonychia, Light Cahill, March Brown, midges, Quill Gordon, Giant Stonefly, terrestrials, Yellow Midge, Yellow Stonefly.

Equipment to Use
Rods: A 3- or 4-weight is ideal for the trout. A 6-weight is more adequate for the 16- to 20-inch "steelhead."
Reels: Standard disc drag.
Lines: Floating to match rod weight.
Leaders: 4x-7x leaders, 9 to 10 feet in length.
Wading: Wet-wading is fine in the warmer months, chest waders are preferable in cooler conditions.

Continued

The author probes a deep run on a lower section of Big Snowbird Creek. Photo by Elizabeth Larson.

Lower Falls is a series of cascades on Big Snowbird Creek and is just upstream of a large waterfall.

predator had followed the path. No snowbirds were sighted, but I heard them along with some chickadees and the wild call of a pileated woodpecker that echoed through the forest.

About three miles from the trailhead, Sassafras Creek crosses the path. This is a popular camping area with good fishing access. Nearby, an old auto relic from an earlier era sits under some bushes, replete with bullet holes. The fly fisher is likely to catch more small rainbows than browns in this stretch of rugged pocket water. On that warm, winter day I observed a cream caddisfly and a fluttering March brown. Other than that, the only hatch activity was some tiny midges. Another half mile on the upstream trail, you hear the rumble of Lower Falls. It is the first of three major waterfalls along the trail. (Lower, Middle, and Upper). Access to the Lower Falls area is precarious. I worked my way down a steep ravine, using rhododendron limbs as hand holds. From the Lower Falls cascades on up, it is wild trout water. The headwaters are located near the Cherohala Skyway (The Dragons Tail), at Hooper Bald. With some seven miles of backcountry stream access, Big Snowbird Creek is almost as remote as neighboring Slickrock Creek. It is considered to be the biggest and one of the best brook trout streams in the state.

Big 'Bow Time

I had heard about the steelhead at Lake Santeetlah. The term "steelhead" refers to the chrome-like silver color of sea-run rainbow trout, which in many coastal streams of the Pacific Northwest, are naturally anadromous, similar to salmon. Here, the "steelhead" are born in the river, migrate to Lake Santeetlah, then migrate back upstream to mate. They are virtually the same species as rainbow trout, and if you landed either one of them you would not complain. Winter is the time to seek them out. There are a few good turnouts near Lake Santeetlah, including a nice little public picnic area. Steelhead prefer deep pockets with boulders. Sometimes you can see them, but catching them is another matter. This is where a good guide can be helpful. A steelhead usually strikes a fly out of irritation, not necessarily because it is hungry. I had plenty of experience with them when I lived in Oregon, where steelhead fishing takes on religious reverence among devotees.

Meanwhile, on my way back to the trailhead, along the high backcountry trail, a blast of feathers startled me, as a ruffed grouse exploded from some nearby cover. I watched as the rusty red bird glided in a curving arc down and over the bare trees and disappeared into the valley below.

To get to Big Snowbird Creek, you need to go to Graham County, and the town of Robbinsville, in extreme western North Carolina. Follow 129 to 143 (Massey Branch). At the "T" stop sign, turn west and follow the Big Snowbird Road signs. About 3/10 mile northwest of Robinson's Grocery, make a hairpin turn back to the left. Continue another mile to a concrete bridge, cross it, and turn right. You are on state road 1120. A sign says "Snowbird Backcountry." This turns into Forest Service Road 75. The gravel road follows the stream until it dead ends at "the Junction" parking area. I highly recommend stopping in at the Cheoah Ranger Station, just off of 143 W on the way in. They have maps and good information on hiking and any tributary closures.

Bonnie and Clyde slept here. Kidding aside, there are remnants of old logging operations and an earlier era along Big Snowbird Creek.

Flies to Use

Drys: Adams, sizes 16-18; Black Beetle, 14-16; Blue Dun Thorax, 18-22; Blue-Winged Olive Parachute, 14-20; Blue Quill, 14-18; Cahill, 14-20; Coffin Fly, 14-18; Dave's Hopper, 12-14; Elk-Hair Caddis, 16-18; Flying Ant, 12-18; Griffith's Glo Bug, 14-18; Gnat, 20; Gray Midge, 18-22; Hendrickson, 14-18; Humpy, 16-18; Inchworm, 14-18; Irresistible, 14-18; Little Yellow Sally, 14-20; March Brown, 16-18; Mosquito, 14-18; Quill Gordon, 12-20; Royal Coachman, 14-18; Royal Wulff, 14-18; Sheep Fly, 14-18; Stimulator, 12-18; Thunderhead, 12-16; Yellow Hammer, 10-14.

Nymphs & Streamers: Brassie, sizes 14-18; Beadhead Pheasant Tail Nymph, 16-18; Beadhead Gold-Ribbed Hare's Ear, 14-16; Bullethead Grasshopper, 10; Copper John, 14-18; Damsel, 14-16; Flashback Hare's Ear Nymph, 14-18; Gray Ghost, 8-12; Little Prince Nymph, 16-18; March Brown Nymph, 16-18; Mickey Finn, 8-10; Muddler Minnow, 6-10; Pat's Nymph;, 18-24; San Juan Worm, 14-16; Scud, 12-18; Sculpin, 6-8; Stone Nymph, 6-10; Woolly Bugger, 6-10; Wickham's Nymph, 12-16.

When to Fish

Sections of Big Snowbird Creek are open to fishing year-round, but during winter it would be advisable to check-in with the Cheoah Ranger Office as well as to study the weather conditions so you do not get socked in.

Season & Limits

The area above The Junction is covered by Wild Trout regulations, which state that you must use a single hook and artificial lures with one hook only. Minimum length is seven inches. The daily creel limit is four, with no closed season. Hatchery regulations prevail below The Junction. The hatchery-supported sections are closed during March. The rest of the year there is no size limit or bait restrictions. The creel limit is seven trout per day. Because regulations are subject to change, you should always consult the NCWRC Regulations. www.ncwildlife.org.

Nearby Fly Fishing

Lake Santeetlah, Big and Little Santeetlah Creeks, Slickrock Creek.

Accommodations & Services

The town of Robbinsville is your best bet for accommodations and services.

Rating

This is a fine destination if you do not mind long hikes or bushwhacking. The trade off is solitude and a wilderness environment in the backcountry. I give it an 8.

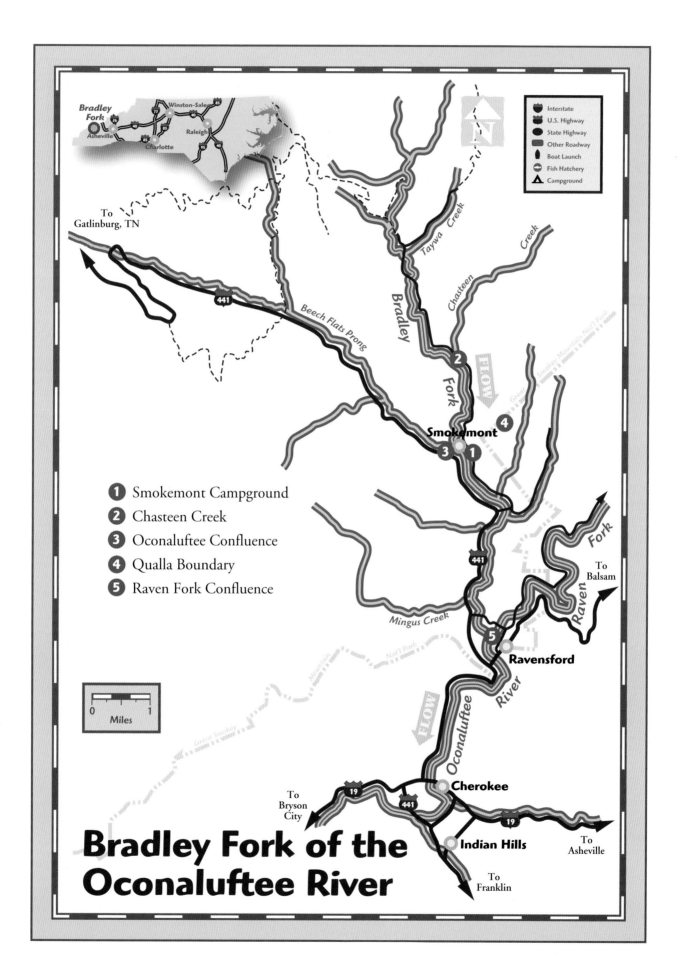

Legend
- Interstate
- U.S. Highway
- State Highway
- Other Roadway
- Boat Launch
- Fish Hatchery
- Campground

Bradley Fork

To Gatlinburg, TN

441

Beech Flats Prong

Taywa Creek

Chasteen Creek

Bradley Fork

Great Smokey Mountain Nat'l Park

Smokemont

3 1

4

1 Smokemont Campground
2 Chasteen Creek
3 Oconaluftee Confluence
4 Qualla Boundary
5 Raven Fork Confluence

441

Mingus Creek

Raven Fork

To Balsam

5

Ravensford

Oconaluftee River

FLOW

Mountain Nat'l Park

Great Smokey

0 Miles 1

To Bryson City

19

441

Cherokee

19

Indian Hills

To Asheville

To Franklin

Bradley Fork of the Oconaluftee River

Bradley Fork, Oconaluftee River

This is an exceptionally beautiful freestone trout stream in an area regarded as sacred by the Cherokee people. It is not difficult to understand why it is held in high regard. Smokemont Campground, on the banks of the Bradley Fork, is an ideal fly-fishing base camp. This Great Smoky Mountain National Park campground occupies the site of a former logging and Civilian Conservation Corps camp. Smokemont is one of the campgrounds that requires a reservation from May 15 through October 31. This fly-fishing mecca is only five miles north of the present-day town of Cherokee. The Bradley Fork Trail, shrouded by red oak, tulip poplar, and river birch, begins nearby as a wide, easy trek that parallels the stream. Just below the campground, the Bradley Fork merges with the Oconaluftee River. Oconaluftee is an Anglicized word that evolved from the Cherokee word that meant "by the

The Bradley Fork flows within the Great Smoky Mountain National Park boundaries. Its confluence with the Oconaluftee lies just below Smokemont Campground.

This brown-trout fingerling from the Bradley Fork is gemlike with its brilliant markings.

A mist shrouds the ancient waters of the Bradley Fork
of the Oconaluftee near Smokemont Campground.

river," referring to the native communities that once stood in this valley. Over time it has become known as the name of the river itself. There is fine fishing both above and alongside the campground. Keep an eye out for elk that have migrated into the area from the Cataloochee Valley. I photographed a young bull as he grazed contentedly in a meadow below the campground near the banks of the Oconaluftee.

As you head upstream a mile or so, on the Bradley Fork Trail beyond the campground, you will encounter Chasteen Creek, a sizable tributary near Backcountry Campsite 50 on the right. Chasteen Creek has its own trail and a mix of rainbows and browns. Continuing upstream, the next tributary is Taywa Creek; beyond here brook trout begin to populate the stream. Some of these smaller tributaries such as Taywa Creek may be closed, so look for postings on the trees and get maps and information from the ranger office or visitor center. Remember that the backcountry campsites require a reservation and may be closed due to bear activity.

Another way to explore the area is to drive north on Newfound Gap Road (U.S. Highway 441). This road follows the Oconaluftee up to the border with Tennessee, providing turnouts and good access. Remember that while the Bradley Fork and Smokemont Campground are near the town of Cherokee, a special tribal-waters permit is not needed as long as you remain in the national park above Smokemont.

Nearby Raven Fork, another good fishable tributary of the Oconaluftee, is within the Qualla Boundary (or reservation), also known as Enterprise Waters, and is managed by the Cherokee People. A state license and trout stamp are not necessary on Enterprise Waters (such as the Raven Fork), however a daily tribal permit is required. Permits are readily available at many businesses in and around the town of Cherokee.

A young bull elk grazes contentedly near the banks of the Oconaluftee near Cherokee.

Types of Fish
Brook trout, browns, and rainbows.

Known Hatches
Blue Quill, Blue-Winged Olive, Brown Dun, Brown Caddis, Brown Drake, Cream Caddis, Cream Cahills, Golden Stones, Giant Stoneflies, Gray Fox, Green Drake, Green Rock Worm, Green Sedge, Hendrickson, Light Cahill, Little Black Winter Stones, Little Brown Stones, March Browns, midges, Olive Caddis, Quill Gordon, Short-horned Sedge, Sulphurs, terrestrials, Tricos, Yellow Sallies, Willowflies.

Equipment to Use
Rods: 3- to 5-weight, 7½ to 9 feet in length.
Reels: Standard mechanical.
Lines: Weight-forward floating, matched to rod.
Leaders: 4x-6x leaders, 9 feet in length.
Wading: Chest waders recommended.

Flies to Use
Drys: Adams, sizes 12-18; Black Beetle, 14-16; Blue Dun Thorax, 18-22; Blue-Winged Olive Parachute, 14-20; Blue Quill, 14-18; Cahill, 14-20; Coffin Fly, 14-18; Dave's Hopper, 12-14; Elk-Hair Caddis, 16-18; Flying Ant, 12-18; Griffith's Glo Bug, 14-18; Gnat, 20; Gray Midge, 18-22; Hendrickson, 14-18; Humpy, 16-18; Inchworm, 14-18; Irresistible, 14-18; Little Yellow Sally, 14-20; March Brown, 16-18; Mosquito, 14-18; Quill Gordon, 12-20; Royal Coachman, 14-18; Royal Wulff, 14-18; Stimulator, 12-18; Thunderhead, 12-16; Yellow Hammer, 10-14; Yellow Palmer, 12-14.

Nymphs & Streamers: Brassie, sizes 14-18; Beadhead Pheasant Tail, 16-18; Beadhead Gold-Ribbed Hare's Ear, 14-16; Bullet Head Grasshopper, 10; Copper John, 14-18; Damsel, 14-16; Flashback Hare's Ear, 14-18; Gray Ghost, 8-12; Little Prince Nymph, 16-18; March Brown Nymph, 16-18; Mickey Finn, 8-10; Muddler Minnow, 6-10; Pat's Nymph, 18-24; San Juan Worm, 14-16; Scud, 12-18; Sculpin, 6-8; Stone Nymph, 6-10; Woolly Bugger, 6-10; Wickham's Nymph, 14-18; Y2k, 12-14; Zonker, 4-10; Zug Bug, 16.

When to Fish
March through early May and September through November are good months but watch the forecast for snow.

Season and Limits
Open year-round. Single hook. Check current regulations. Stop by park office to find out which tributaries are open.

Nearby Fly Fishing
Oconaluftee, Raven Fork, Nantahala River, Deep Creek.

Accommodations & Services
Smokemont is a fine base camp close to everything, with the towns of Cherokee and Bryson City both within a short drive.

Rating
On a good day Bradley Fork rates an 8.

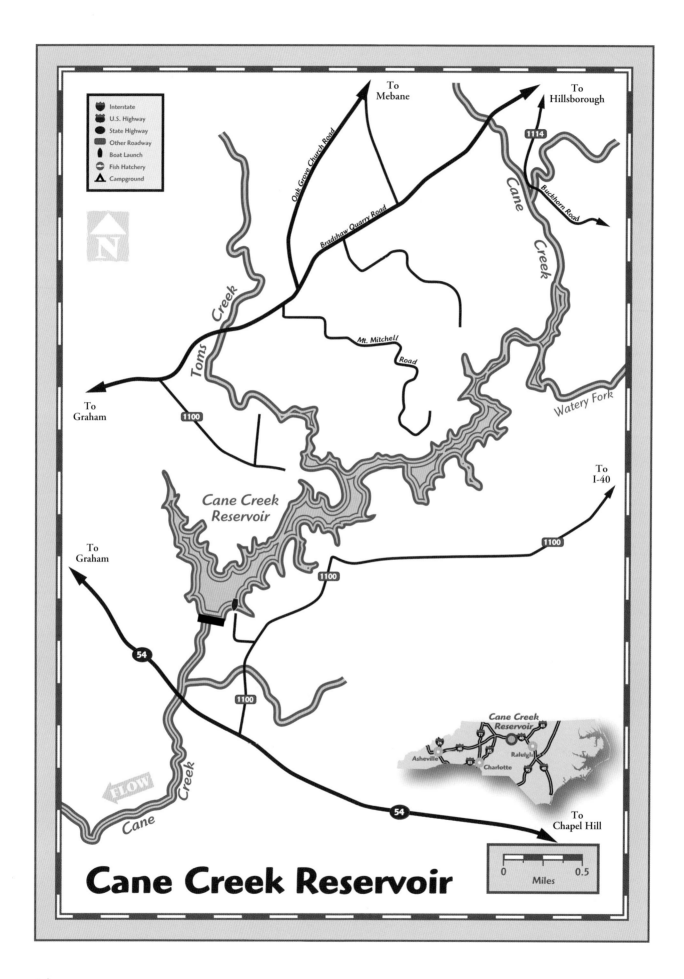

Legend:
- Interstate
- U.S. Highway
- State Highway
- Other Roadway
- Boat Launch
- Fish Hatchery
- Campground

N

To Mebane

To Hillsborough

1114

Oak Grove Church Road

Bradshaw Quarry Road

Cane Creek

Buckhorn Road

Toms Creek

Mt. Mitchell Road

Watery Fork

To Graham

1100

To I-40

Cane Creek Reservoir

To Graham

1100

1100

54

1100

FLOW

Cane Creek

Cane Creek Reservoir

Asheville

Raleigh

Charlotte

To Chapel Hill

54

0   Miles   0.5

Cane Creek Reservoir

Cane Creek Reservoir

entrally located in the state near Chapel Hill, Cane Creek is a relaxing place where it is not unusual to catch bass numbering to double digits. Ideally situated for small-boat anglers, the setting is peaceful and pastoral. I first learned about it while enjoying *Hank Parker's Outdoor Magazine* television show that featured former University of North Carolina Tarheel and NBA star Eric Montross. Several impounded tributaries, including Cane Creek, Caterpillar Creek, Toms Creek, Turkey Hill Creek, and Watery Fork, contributed to the creation of Cane Creek Reservoir in 1989. Early morning, when the wind is down and the only noise is the slap on the water from a vigorous surface strike, is my favorite time to fish here.

Big flies, such as poppers and dragonfly and damselfly imitations, work well. Chartreuse seems to be the go-to color. Cruise the edges and cast your fly near stumps, logs, or drop-offs. Later in the day, try beadhead Woolly Buggers or crawfish patterns. This body of water is a reservoir that is controlled by Orange Water and Sewer

The author casts near the boat launch at Cane Creek Reservoir near Chapel Hill, NC. Photo by Tammy Pegram.

The approach to Cane Creek boat landing. Electric motors and non-trailered boats are allowed at Cane Creek Reservoir near Chapel Hill.

The author looks to initiate some top water action in the morning at Cane Creek, when the lake is calm. Photo by Tammy Pegram.

Authority (OWASA), which provides water for the neighboring communities of Chapel Hill and Carrboro. Water quality control is carefully scrutinized.

Electric trolling motors are allowed but gas motors are not. You can bring a non-trailered boat or rent a small rowboat, canoe, and even a trolling motor. If you bring your own boat and motor, a warden will inspect them to make sure the prop or boat is clean of mud and vegetation. There are a couple of caveats. Cane Creek is only open Fridays and Saturdays. There is a launch fee for Orange County residents with their own boat, and a slightly higher fee if you are from another county. The boat ramp gets a little busy but the 540-acre reservoir is much bigger than it looks. There are nineteen miles of shoreline so with a little effort, you can find your own little cove. The average depth is about seventeen feet. The northern side of the lake has some good stump and log structure that holds pan fish and creates good cover for bucketheads. I have rarely if ever seen another fly fisher. Most of the folks here use spinning gear, some use live bait, and many sit anchored in one place for long periods. For more information, call the lake warden's office at (919) 942-5790, the OWASA offices at (919) 968-4421, or go to www.owasa.org.

From I-40, travel southward on N.C. Highway 54 about twelve miles, approximately 1.7 miles past the Orange County line. The gated entrance is on the left. From Carrboro it is eleven miles to the west on N.C. 54.

Cane Creek gets no fishing pressure during the week so Saturdays yield some nice quality fish.

Wildlife is abundant at Cane Creek including many species of birds such as this Greater Yellowlegs.

Types of Fish
Largemouth bass, crappie, catfish, bluegills, and sunfish.

Equipment to Use
Rods: 5- to 9-weight, 8 to 9 1/2 feet in length.
Reels: Mechanical and palm.
Lines: Weight-forward floating matched to rod or short sink-tip.
Wading: This water is more suited to a small boat, canoe, or kayak.

Flies to Use
Drys: Surface flies including poppers and sliders.

Nymphs & Streamers: Big streamers. Try Bachmann's Crawdad Tan/Brown, size 4; Beadhead Goldilox, 4-8; Bullethead Grasshopper, 8-10; Clouser Minnow, 4-8; Mc2 Crayfish, 4-8; Muddler Minnow, 1-6; Sculpin, 6-8; Woolly Bugger, 4-8; Zonker, 4-8.

When to Fish
Spring is excellent, as is fall.

Season and Limits
March to November (exact dates will vary from year to year) from 6:30 am to 6 pm, Fridays and Saturdays only, check current schedule. (919) 942-5790 or ccreek@owasa.org. North Carolina fishing-license guidelines are applicable.

Nearby Fly Fishing
University Lake is a smaller, older, yet similar OWASA impoundment located nearby. Open Fridays through Sundays, (919) 942-8007 or ulake@owasa.org.

Accommodations and Services
The towns of Carrboro and Chapel Hill are close by and offer lots of options.

Rating
Because of the light fly-fishing pressure during each week, lack of noisy gas motors, and the size and quantity of bass, I rate Cane Creek Reservoir a 9.

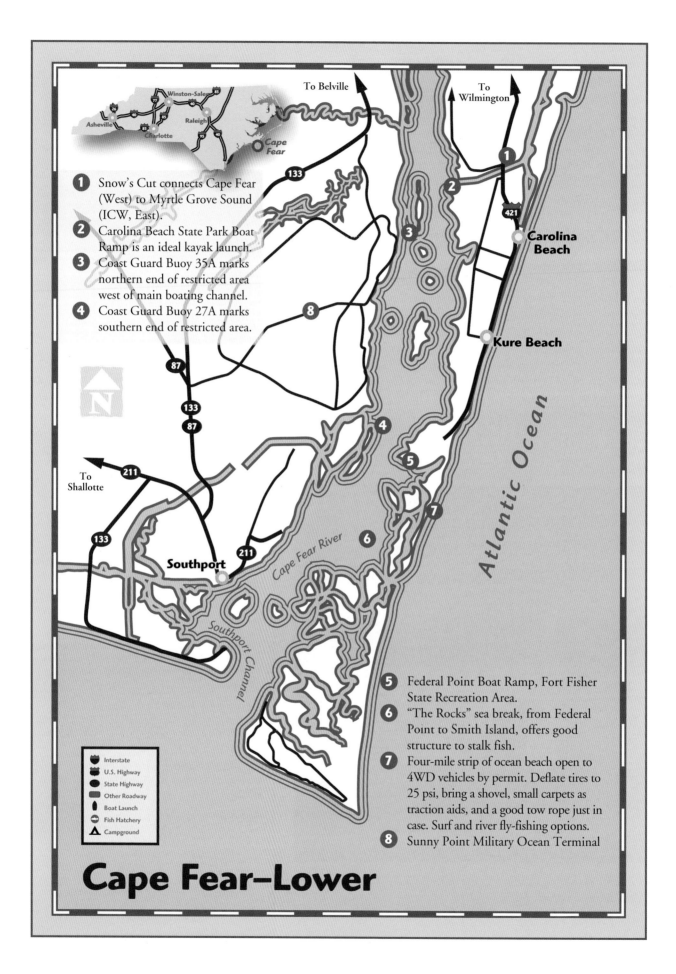

① Snow's Cut connects Cape Fear (West) to Myrtle Grove Sound (ICW, East).

② Carolina Beach State Park Boat Ramp is an ideal kayak launch.

③ Coast Guard Buoy 35A marks northern end of restricted area west of main boating channel.

④ Coast Guard Buoy 27A marks southern end of restricted area.

⑤ Federal Point Boat Ramp, Fort Fisher State Recreation Area.

⑥ "The Rocks" sea break, from Federal Point to Smith Island, offers good structure to stalk fish.

⑦ Four-mile strip of ocean beach open to 4WD vehicles by permit. Deflate tires to 25 psi, bring a shovel, small carpets as traction aids, and a good tow rope just in case. Surf and river fly-fishing options.

⑧ Sunny Point Military Ocean Terminal

To Belville

To Wilmington

Carolina Beach

Kure Beach

Atlantic Ocean

Cape Fear River

Southport Channel

Southport

To Shallotte

Interstate
U.S. Highway
State Highway
Other Roadway
Boat Launch
Fish Hatchery
Campground

Cape Fear–Lower

Cape Fear— Lower

Note the dark color camouflage of this flounder, which matches the dark sand of Lower Cape Fear.

The sun rose over the salt marsh, while on the dock across from our boat, a group of folks and their dog prepared for a day of crabbing. Capt. Matt Wirt's 18-foot flats boat idled as we loaded our fly rods and gear.

My friend Joseph Corso was down from Portland, Oregon, to make the trip. An accomplished steelheader, he and I had shared many adventures in places such as the Deschutes River Canyon in central Oregon back in the nineties.

Not far from our put-in site, I could see large mounds—remnants of Fort Fisher's Confederate earthworks during the Civil War. At the dawn of the 19th century, Wilmington was North Carolina's largest city and a busy shipping port. Cape Fear's headwaters begin near Greensboro as two distinct streams, the Haw River and the Deep River. The Cape Fear runs southeast for 200 miles from the piedmont of North Carolina, through Fayetteville and the sand

Joseph Corso strips line along the salt marsh.

Stalking redfish requires accurate casting.

hills region, widening as it receives the Northeast Cape Fear in the coastal plain near Wilmington. For about fifteen miles from the city to the mouth, the river gradually becomes a wide estuary and a segment of the Intracoastal Waterway.

On this fine day we were looking for a mixed bag of fishing opportunity. Captain Matt eased us out onto the calm water of Buzzard's Bay from Federal Point. Egrets flushed and pelicans flew in formation just overhead. It was high tide. A disturbance in the water came into view like some sort of a long straight riptide. Our side was calm, the far side was rougher. "We're getting ready to take a shortcut and cross a wall," Captain Matt informed us as he let up on the throttle and raised the motor. The nearly invisible 3.3 mile wall is also known as *The Rocks,* constructed in the late 1800s by the U.S. Army Corps of Engineers as a swash defense dam. Later at low tide it was clearly visible. It resembled a long slick jetty that anglers fish off of.

In the distance we could see the lighthouses of Bald Head and Oak Island. We fished along the grassy fringes and oyster bed drop-offs. Then Joseph had a hook up that bent his 8-weight in half. After a good battle he landed a very nice spotted flounder on a Matt Wirt variation of a white Clouser Minnow. We continued through the maze of salt marsh taking turns, missing, and spooking a couple of redfish. At one point a black-tip shark showed up in casting range but bypassed my fly. As the tide dropped we worked our way to a deep hole known to hold speckled trout. Switching to a 12-foot sinking-tip line I made about thirty casts and eventually landed a nice fish. A boat is your best bet for fishing the Lower Cape Fear although there is some fishable shoreline near the small boat dock as well as the rock wall during the falling tide. Careful though, it is quite slick. A good guide such as Capt. Matt Wirt will know exactly where to go and what is biting. The Federal Point Ramp at Fort Fisher can be reached from the town of Kure Beach on U.S. 421 South 4.5 miles just past the Ferry Terminal.

A wealth of bird life populates the Lower Cape Fear, including the ruddy turnstone.

Types of Fish
There is a nice variety including redfish, bluefish, speckled trout, flounder, black drum, and ladyfish.

Known Baitfish
Anglers on the Lower Cape Fear can expect finger mullet, menhaden, other small baitfish, shrimp, and crabs.

Equipment to Use
Rods: 6- to 9-weight rods, 9 to 9½ feet in length.
Reels: Mechanical and large arbor reels.
Lines: Intermediate floating line, 10- to 15-foot sinking-tip lines for sea trout.
Leaders: 0x to 2x leaders, 9 feet in length (wire leaders should be used for bluefish).
Wading: Anglers can use chest waders as well as canoes, kayaks, and other shallow-draft boats.

Flies to Use
Bend Back, sizes 1/0-2; Bruce's Crystal Shrimp, 1/0; Clouser Minnow, 2/0-4; DuBiel's Finesse Fly, 2-4; DuBiel's Lil' Hadden, 1/0-2; DuBiel's Red-Ducer, 1/0-2; Lefty's Deceiver, 2/0-2; Lefty's Half & Half, 2/0-2; Popovic's Surf Candy, 1/0; Tommy's Crease Fly, 2/0-2; Tommy's Eel Fly, 2/0-1/0; Trow's Minnow, 3/0-6; Wirt's Redfish Rattler, 2/0-2.

When to Fish
Spring and fall are the best times to fish, but summer and winter can produce as well.

Season & Limits
Open all year. Consult the North Carolina Division of Marine Fisheries in Wilmington (910) 796-7215, and ask for a copy of their most recent saltwater regulations for full details.

Nearby Fly Fishing
Carolina Beach (see pages 46–49), Wrightsville Beach, Masonboro Inlet.

Accommodations & Services
There is a lot to choose from at Carolina Beach, Wrightsville Beach, Kure Beach, and Wilmington.

Rating
This is a fine area to explore and fish and easily rates an 8.

Sea trout prefer deeper water so you'll want to use sinking lines.

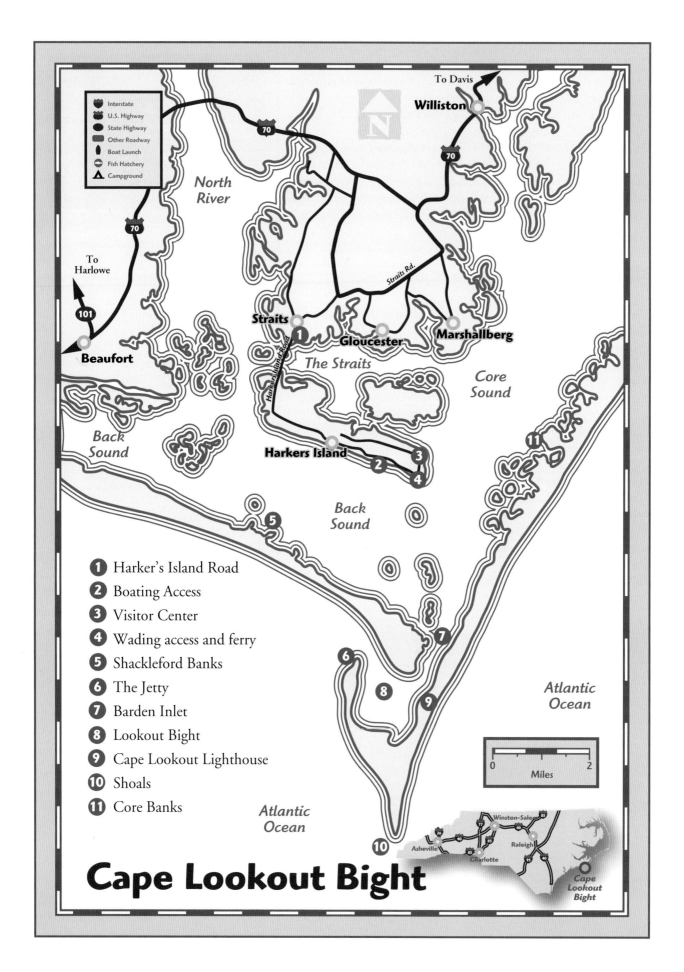

Legend:
- Interstate
- U.S. Highway
- State Highway
- Other Roadway
- Boat Launch
- Fish Hatchery
- Campground

North River

To Davis

Williston

70

70

To Harlowe

101

Beaufort

Straits Rd.

Straits

1

Gloucester

Marshallberg

The Straits

Core Sound

Back Sound

Harkers Island

3

2

4

11

Back Sound

5

7

6

8

9

Atlantic Ocean

1 Harker's Island Road
2 Boating Access
3 Visitor Center
4 Wading access and ferry
5 Shackleford Banks
6 The Jetty
7 Barden Inlet
8 Lookout Bight
9 Cape Lookout Lighthouse
10 Shoals
11 Core Banks

Atlantic Ocean

10

0   Miles   2

Cape Lookout Bight

Winston-Salem
Asheville
Raleigh
Charlotte
Cape Lookout Bight

Cape Lookout Bight

The Cape Lookout area is a unique place. The iconic black-and-white diamond-patterned lighthouse stands on a spit of sandy land that is a curving barrier island. From above, the lower end resembles a hook. Inside the hook, or bight, conditions are usually a bit calmer than outside the bight, and that creates opportunity for anglers. This is a fabled area, populated with porpoises and even wild ponies on nearby Shackelford Banks. There also is a rich variety of species to target with a fly rod—speckled sea trout, king mackerel, Spanish mackerel, flounder, bluefish, and false albacore also known as little tunny, fat Albert, or just plain albie.

Albies are members of the tuna family and are known for their line-ripping explosiveness. Ten-weight rods are recommended for these powerful fish. Albies are visual hunters and prefer clear water conditions. Look for a water temperatures between 58 and 64 degrees. In addition to a favorable wind, anglers will need to find the baitfish that attract this predator, which feed primarily on menhaden and silversides or glass minnows (anchovies). Observe the birds. Active gulls are the key here, and they will flock to the

A boat angler inspects a Barden Inlet albie.

David Dow returns every fall to pursue false albacore near Cape Lookout.

David Dow casting into the action.

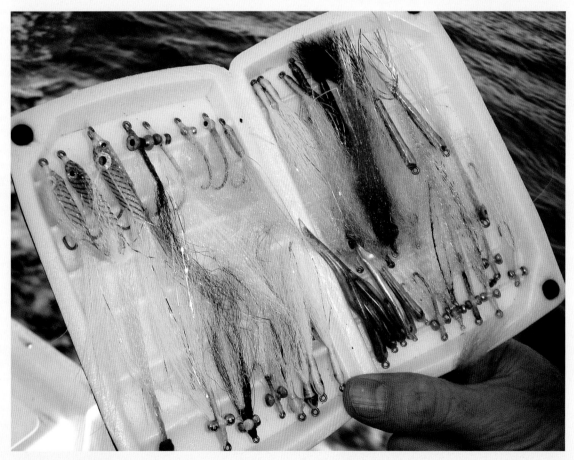

A selection of colorful saltwater flies.

scraps of menhaden that albies leave behind as they corral the bait and attack. Often the bait balls may attract other predators including sharks. Make sure you are using stout fluorocarbon or steel leader. Cast to the froth with a sinking-tip line. Sturdy backing will be required for the long runs. The fish are in a feeding frenzy so there is no use in trying to lead them with your cast. Once you begin your retrieve, strip fast and manage your line, because if you hook an albie, you will be in for a fight!

Wading anglers are not uncommon on the edges of the bight. Many fly fishermen here use a stripping basket to hold their fly lines. The jetty is a great place to cast for bluefish, reds, or speckled trout using 7- or 8-weight rods with sinking lines. A good sturdy boat and an experienced captain or guide are a good idea. Glass minnow or silverside streamers are the best choice for a fly.

David Dow is a friend and avid fly fisher who has years of experience on these waters. One October afternoon he took us out near the shoals on the seaward side of Cape Point (the Hook) after we spotted some bird activity. Before long the relaxed rolling waves became very large swells, and it was all we could do to keep the bow level. Eventually our skilled skipper, Dow, was able to safely turn the craft around, and we headed to the calmer waters of Barden's Inlet. It was definitely a white-knuckled adventure I will not soon forget.

Another fishing buddy and guide, Jeff Wilkins, summed up the chances for engaging false albacore by making an analogy to a typical baseball player's batting average. He said if you go out on three or four different days during October or November and conditions are right, you might get into some fish on one of those days. So a .250 or .333 average is about what you might expect. But even if you don't find the albies, the scenery and variety of fish, including occasional ocean redfish, make visiting the Hook worth the trip.

Nearby Harkers Island offers marinas with boating access and a visitor center that are worth checking out. Numerous ferries, including one operated by the National Park Service, provide shuttles for anglers who might want to venture out to the Hook on foot. To get there, travel eastward on highway 70 from Morehead City or Beaufort and south right on Harkers Island Road (SR 1335).

David Dow displays a fine "fat Albert."

Types of Fish

This area is most famous for the false albacore runs that begin in October and continue through November. There are also speckled trout, weakfish, cobia, king mackerel, Spanish mackerel, striped bass, sharks, bluefish, flounder, and redfish.

Equipment to Use

Rods: 7- to 10-weight rods, 9 to 9½ feet in length.
Reels: Mechanical drag and large-arbor reels.
Lines: Intermediate floating line, 10- to 15-foot, 350- to 400-grain sinking-tip for sea trout and false albacore.
Leaders: 0x to 2x leaders, 5 to 10 feet in length (wire leaders should be used for bluefish).
Wading: Anglers can use chest waders.
Boat access: Seaworthy boats and kayaks.

Flies to Use

Bend Back, sizes 1/0-2; Bruce's Crystal Shrimp, 1/0; Clouser Minnow, 2/0-4; DuBiel's Finesse Fly, 2-4; DuBiel's Lil'Hadden, 1/0-2; DuBiel's Red-Ducer, 1/0-2; Lefty's Deceiver, 2/0-2; Lefty's Half & Half, 2/0-2; Popovics's Surf Candy, 1/0; Tommy's Crease Fly, 2/0-2; Tommy's Eel Fly, 2/0-1/0; Trow's Minnow, 3/0-6; Wirt's Redfish Rattler, 2/0-2.

When to Fish

Spring and fall are the best times to fish. October through November is the best time for false albacore.

Seasons & Limits

Obtain a copy of the regulations for slot limits from the North Carolina Wildlife Resources Commission available at most tackle and fly shops.

Nearby Fly Fishing

Beaufort Inlet, Intracoastal Waterway, Core Banks, Shackelford Island, and Harkers Island.

Accommodations & Services

Morehead City, Beaufort, and Harkers Island offer a wide variety of resources.

Rating

The Cape Lookout area rates an 8, but when the fish are in, this is the place to be.

Wild ponies graze near the channel on Shackelford Banks.

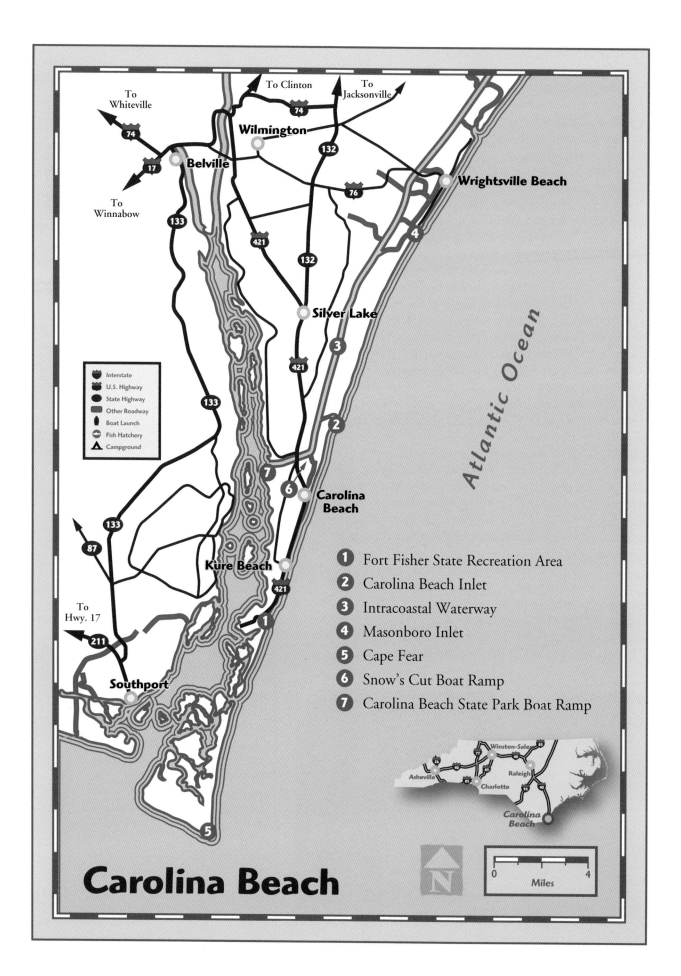

To Clinton

To Jacksonville

To Whiteville

To Winnabow

Wilmington

Belville

Wrightsville Beach

Interstate
U.S. Highway
State Highway
Other Roadway
Boat Launch
Fish Hatchery
Campground

Silver Lake

Atlantic Ocean

Carolina Beach

Kure Beach

To Hwy. 17

Southport

1 Fort Fisher State Recreation Area
2 Carolina Beach Inlet
3 Intracoastal Waterway
4 Masonboro Inlet
5 Cape Fear
6 Snow's Cut Boat Ramp
7 Carolina Beach State Park Boat Ramp

Winston-Salem
Asheville
Raleigh
Charlotte
Carolina Beach

Carolina Beach

N

0   Miles   4

Carolina Beach

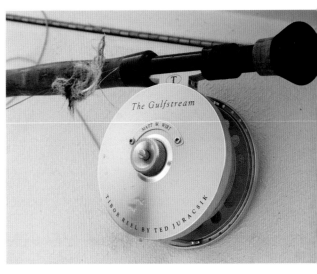

A ridge of dark clouds menaced the horizon as we motored from the Snow's Cut boat ramp and out to sea. We were aiming to catch shark on the fly, but a big storm had hit two days before. In the aftermath of the storm, we were not yet sure if we would find shrimp trawlers on the water. And trawlers were key to our hopes, because we hoped to target sharks as they keyed on a trawler's by-catch.

Plying the by-catch is the same idea as fishing a chum line, only the shrimpers are creating the chum line for you. Some shrimp captains are not keen on having anglers behind their boat, but my guide, Capt. Matt Wirt, has established relationships with a few shrimpers. So, we hoped to find a friendly trawler, and a bevy of bird activity behind the boat, which usually means sharks are having a feeding frenzy.

It was early morning off the coast of Carolina Beach in Captain Wirt's 22-foot Ranger bay boat. The first trawler we saw appeared to be heading back to port, but before long we found an active shrimper with plenty of bird activity, including a few telltale

Tools of the trade: a mighty fly rod and reel, stout leader, and a well-honed shark fly.

Captain Matt Wirt with a 72-pound blacktip caught behind a trawler just off of Carolina Beach.

*Capt. Matt Wirt battles a blacktip shark
he hooked behind a shrimp trawler.*

dorsal fins. Captain Wirt picked up one of his 12-weight fly rods and offered me the first cast, I deferred to him, as I wanted to get some photos.

The strike zone for a shark is the area in front of its nose, where it can see the fly and move toward it easily, as sharks close their eyes when they open their mouths to bite. And after just a few vigorous double-hauls, Captain Wirt made a perfect cast into the frothy water, and we were rewarded with a deep bend in the rod and a suddenly taut and outgoing line. This was not one of the little ten-pound dogfish sharks familiar to Carolina surf and pier fishermen, no—this was Jaws Junior. The creature made numerous runs, a couple of spectacular leaps, and reeling him in was hard work. Captain Wirt handed me the rod and I found out for myself—it was the most powerful fish I have ever felt on a fly rod. After battling for another 15 minutes, I conveniently offered Captain Wirt control so I could get some close-up shots of the splashy landing.

Once he had that blacktip under control, he cautiously lip gaffed it and somehow heaved him onto the boat. Much to my amazement, he hoisted the carnivorous creature onto his lap. Obviously Captain Wirt knew what he was doing. Later he told me that he has successfully released hundreds of sharks.

He knows, because he has re-caught many a tagged shark as part of a tagging program. Most the time he is able to release the hooks with pliers, or a de-hooking device, lifting them out carefully behind the gills or with a lip gaff. If he cannot get to the hook, he cuts the wire that will rust out in a few days.

A good look at the sleek shape of a blacktip shark.

Types of Fish

Shark species you can target here include hammerhead, blacktip, dusky, sandbar, Atlantic sharpnose, spinner, bull, and sand tiger. Other game fish include, red drum, bluefish, king mackerel, Spanish mackerel, speckled sea trout, flounder, and croaker.

Equipment to Use

Rods: For sharks up to 100 pounds, stout 10- to 12-weight rods are recommended; a 13- to 14-weight rod can handle up to 150 pounds. For redfish, bluefish, and mackerel, 7- to 9-weights are preferred.

Reels: Non-corrosive large-arbor reels with a good disc drag.

Lines: Floating, saltwater taper, weight-forward, and intermediate lines to match rod weight.

Leaders: For sharks; 2½ feet of 60- 80-pound-test hard mono on the butt section, followed by a 2½ foot mid-section of 20- to 60-pound mono, and then a bite tippet constructed of 18 inches of either 60-pound-test stranded wire or coated stainless-steel tied with an Albright knot. For mackerel, use a lighter wire shock tippet with lighter mono such as 20- to 30-pound test.

Boat: A good bay boat is advisable, ideally with a captain who knows these waters.

Flies to Use

Bend Back, sizes 1/0-2; Blados's Crease Fly, 3/0-4; Blanton's Sar Mul Mac, 3/0; Chocklett's Gummy Minnow, 2/0; Clouser Minnow, 2/0-2; Cowen's Baitfish, 1/0; Dubiel's Lil'Hadden, 1/0-2; Dubiel's Red-Ducer, 3/0-1/0; Eel Fly, 2/0-1/0; Dubiel's Foxy Minnow, 2/0-2; Lefty's Half and Half, 2/0-2; Lefty's Deceiver, 2/0-2; Walt's Saltwater Popper (Chartreuse), 2/0-2; Wirt's Redfish Slider, 2/0-2; Wirt's Shark Fly 7/0-5/0.

When to Fish

Spring, summer, and fall are best.

Season & Limits

Consult North Carolina regulations regarding slot limits.

Nearby Fly Fishing

Wrightsville Beach area, Intracoastal Waterway, Cape Fear—Lower, see pages 38–41.

Accommodations & Services

Wilmington, Carolina Beach, and Kure Beach offer a wealth of services.

Helpful Websites

www.reel-adventure.com/
www.wilmingtonandbeaches.com
www.intracoastalangler.com
www.ncparks.gov

Rating

My shark fishing trip with Captain Wirt was a very unique and educational experience with great action on the fly rod. Based on that experience, I would have to rate it a 10.

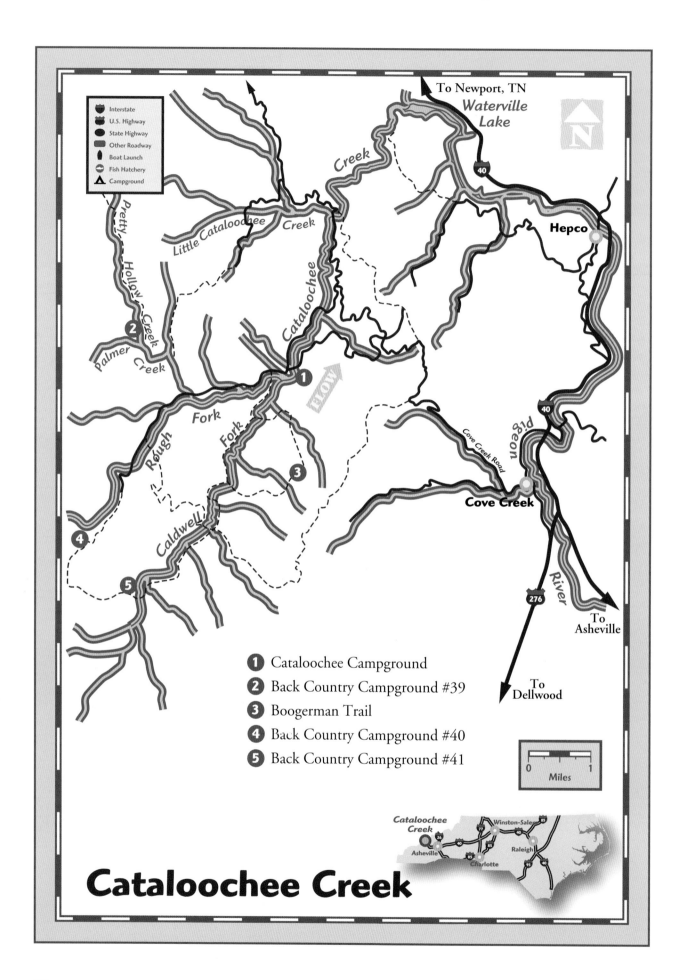

To Newport, TN

Waterville Lake

Creek

40

Hepco

Little Cataloochee Creek

Pretty Hollow Creek

Palmer Creek

Cataloochee Creek

FLOW

Rough Fork

Fork

Cove Creek Road

Pigeon River

40

276

Cove Creek

To Asheville

To Dellwood

Caldwell

Legend
- Interstate
- U.S. Highway
- State Highway
- Other Roadway
- Boat Launch
- Fish Hatchery
- Campground

1 Cataloochee Campground
2 Back Country Campground #39
3 Boogerman Trail
4 Back Country Campground #40
5 Back Country Campground #41

0 — Miles — 1

Cataloochee Creek

Asheville • Winston-Salem • Raleigh • Charlotte

Cataloochee Creek

Cataloochee Creek

The author hooked this brown trout near a submerged stump on Cataloochee Creek about a mile from the campground.

Bull elk in velvet are common sites each spring in the Cataloochee Valley, since these big members of the deer family were reintroduced into the Smokies more than a decade ago.

The morning mist over the mountain meadows reminded me of a magnificent scene from Montana or Colorado. Tan shapes, grazing elk that seem to be thriving, punctuated the landscape, which is surrounded by some of the highest mountain peaks in the Southeast. The successful reintroduction of elk into the area in 2001 and 2002 has added a wonderful spirit of wildness. On that May morning something else moved through the tall grass—a coyote perhaps? No, it was a turkey. After some quiet observation in the serene Cataloochee Valley it is not unusual to spot the toms as they strut about, putting on their annual display for the hens. Soon I set out from my camp along the Caldwell Fork of Cataloochee Creek to see what trout I could fool.

Exit 20 west from I-40 will take you to Cove Creek Road where you turn to follow a winding, partially gravel road that works its way over a ridge and into the Cataloochee Valley. Another route is going north on Highway 276 from Maggie Valley and turning left on Cove Creek Road. This was the route that hunters of the Cherokee Nation once used and was later used by settlers in horse-drawn wagons. This Smoky Mountain valley is dotted with vintage farm buildings that offer a glimpse into the past. There is a nice little campground that makes a perfect base camp.

Cataloochee Creek is one of the author's favorite streams in North Carolina. Here you'll find solitude, serenity, wildlife, and great fishing.

The Cataloochee Valley is a wildlife bonanza. In addition to elk, the meadows are full of great trout food such as grasshoppers, crickets, and ants.

Jonathan Williamson battles a burly trout in the Caldwell Fork of the Cataloochee Creek.

During day one, I tried to match the stonefly hatch on the main stem of Cataloochee Creek, a small to medium-size stream for the Smokies. I threw a lot of yellow patterns such as size 14 Stimulators and Humpies. Many small gemlike brookies responded, and I started thinking that the little natives were all I was going to catch. That night my camp was cold and drizzly but music from another camp wafted down like smoke from a distant fire. I went to investigate and happened upon a gathering of musicians under a pop-up canopy. An upright bass player, a mandolin player, two guitarists, and a banjo picker composed the band called Cold Mountain. I stayed for several traditional songs and found myself grinning while watching them picking. A young girl, no older than nine years old, sang in harmony with her granddad. It was a warm display of tradition and poise. Overall, the encounter with those musical folks had made a dreary night quite delightful.

Next day, I hit the creek fresh, with a new strategy. Although the water level was up, the creek was as clear as tea and still fishable. Overcast conditions helped me decide how to approach the water. I tied a size 12 Wickham's Nymph to my tippet—this pattern is a secret weapon created by an acquaintance of mine from Reidsville. I met "Uncle Cecil" Chapman at meetings of the Nat Greene Flyfishers, an affiliate of Trout Unlimited and the Federation of Fly Fishers based in the Greensboro, North Carolina. Chapman had created this fly based on his study of an English dry-fly pattern that had lots of moving parts. Anyway, it worked, and I was able to land a fine brown trout as well as a few feisty rainbows. There is nothing like having confidence in a fly. It always seems to make a difference.

There are several other tributaries worth exploring in the valley. Cataloochee Creek is formed by the confluence of Palmer and Rough Fork near the Caldwell homestead. Pretty Hollow is a tributary of Palmer Creek. Little Cataloochee Creek is somewhat more difficult to access, and at the time of this writing, the road access bridge was closed. Be sure to check for postings from park rangers for updated stream closures and bear activity.

Brilliantly colored brook trout are abundant in the streams of the Cataloochee Valley.

Types of Fish
Rainbows, brook trout, and browns.

Known Hatches
Baetis, Black Caddis, Black Stonefly, Blue Quill, Blue-Winged Olive, Cream Midge, Gray Caddis, Gray Fox, Green Drake, Hendrickson, Isonychia, Light Cahill, March Brown, midge, Quill Gordon, Giant Stonefly, terrestrials, Yellow Midge, Yellow Stonefly.

Equipment to Use
Rods: 2- to 4-weight; 7 to 8 feet in length.
Reels: Mechanical and palm.
Lines: Floating to match rod weight.
Leaders: 4x to 6x, 9 feet in length.
Wading: Chest waders.

Flies to Use
Drys: Adams, sizes 16-18; Black Beetle, 14-16; Blue Dun Thorax, 18-22; Blue-Winged Olive Parachute, 14-20; Blue Quill, 14-18; Cahill, 14-20; Coffin Fly, 14-18; Dave's Hopper, 12-14; Elk-Hair Caddis, 16-18; Flying Ant, 12-18; Griffith's Glo Bug, 14-18; Gnat, 20; Gray Midge, 18-22; Hendrickson, 14-18; Humpy, 16-18; Inchworm, 14-18; Irresistible, 14-18; Little Yellow Sally, 14-20; March Brown, 16-18; Mosquito, 14-18; Quill Gordon, 12-20; Royal Coachman, 14-18; Royal Wulff, 14-18; Stimulator, 12-18; Thunderhead, 12-16; Yellow Hammer, 10-14.

Nymph & Streamers: Brassie, sizes 14-18; Beadhead Pheasant Tail, 16-18; Beadhead Gold Ribbed Hare's Ear, 14-16; Bullethead Grasshopper, 10; Copper John, 14-18; Damsel, 14-16; Flashback Hare's Ear, 14-18; Gray Ghost, 8-12; Little Prince Nymph, 16-18; March Brown Nymph, 16-18; Mickey Finn, 8-10; Muddler Minnow, 6-10; Pat's Nymph, 18-24; San Juan Worm, 14-16; Scud, 12-18; Sculpin, 6-8; Stone Nymph, 6-10; Woolly Bugger, 6-10.

When to Fish
Like most Smoky Mountain streams, Cataloochee Creek and the tributaries fish best in spring and fall.

Season & Limits
Fishing is permitted year-round in the park with a single hook; an artificial fly with up to two flies on the leader. Catch and release is recommended. Always check current regulations.

Nearby Fly Fishing
Big Creek

Accommodations & Services
Cataloochee Campground is an ideal base camp with 27 first-come, first-served campsites. There are a few backcountry sites as well. Campsite 40 is on Rough Fork, 41 is on the Caldwell Fork. Campsite 39 is near the confluence of Pretty Hollow and Palmer Creek. Maggie Valley offers motels and stores about an hour away.

Rating
Because of the beauty, the wildness and solitude, not to mention fishability, Cataloochee Creek is truly one of North Carolina's gems. I rate it a solid 9.

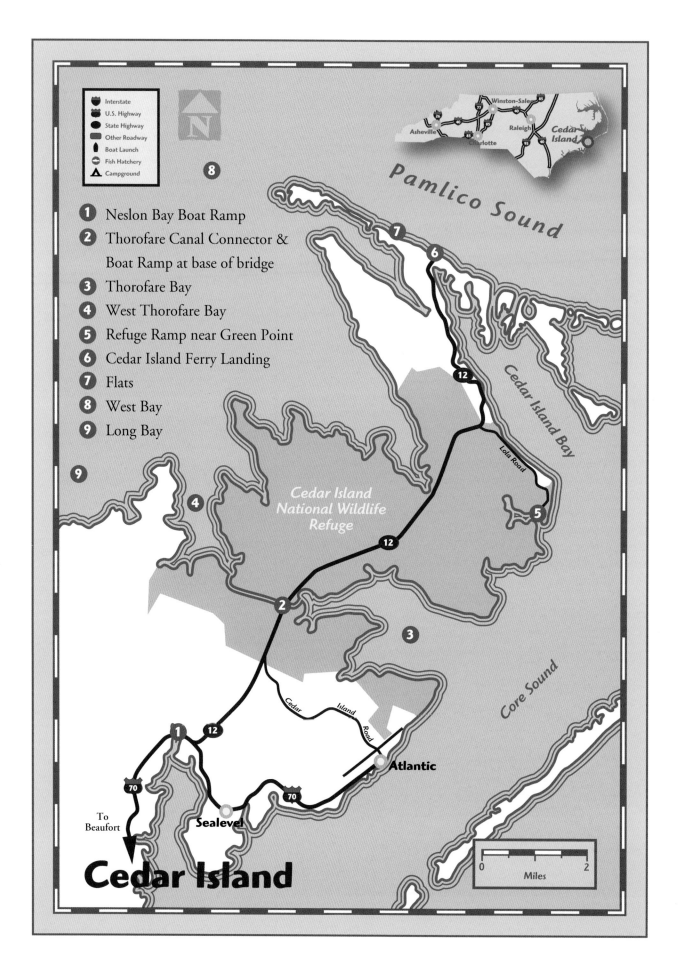

Legend:
- Interstate
- U.S. Highway
- State Highway
- Other Roadway
- Boat Launch
- Fish Hatchery
- Campground

1. Neslon Bay Boat Ramp
2. Thorofare Canal Connector & Boat Ramp at base of bridge
3. Thorofare Bay
4. West Thorofare Bay
5. Refuge Ramp near Green Point
6. Cedar Island Ferry Landing
7. Flats
8. West Bay
9. Long Bay

Pamlico Sound

Cedar Island Bay

Lola Road

Cedar Island National Wildlife Refuge

Core Sound

Cedar Island Road

Atlantic

To Beaufort

Sealevel

Cedar Island

0 Miles 2

Cedar Island

This quiet little fishing village at the southern end of the Pamlico Sound bills itself as the Gateway to the Outer Banks. Tarpon roll around the flats in June, and bluefish, redfish, "specks" (the local term for speckled sea trout), grey trout, ladyfish (like miniature, acrobatic tarpon), flounder, croaker, spot, and kings are seasonal residents. Relaxed and not anywhere near as commercial as other fishing focal points, Cedar Island is a nice escape with only a few hundred permanent residents. It is a stark contrast to the more densely inhabited Morehead City area, which is about 40 miles to the southeast.

Blowin' in the Wind

The Cedar Island Wildlife Refuge consists primarily of saltwater marsh lined with pine and oak trees. Nearly 15,000 acres of marsh provide good inshore fishing for anglers with shallow-draft boats. Most of the waters in the surrounding coves and sound are no deeper than 20 feet. Sea kayaking has caught on here. Thorofare, West, and Long bays provide ideal settings for observing wildlife and finding seclusion with a fly rod. Cordgrass and black needle rush provide a rich habitat for the fish and fowl. Migrant ducks such as redheads, surf scoters, buffleheads, and canvasbacks flock here in large numbers. Nesting water birds you might see include ibis, herons, and skimmers.

One of the biggest challenges to fly fishers is a four-letter word: wind. Of course it is the draw for kite boarders, wind surfers, and sailboat enthusiasts who take advantage of the wide-open spaces.

Water, water everywhere and often quite windy.

Red drum are an ever-popular fly-fishing quarry in and around the saltwater marshes of Cedar Island.

The Cedar Island Wildlife Refuge is ideally suited to kayaks and shallow-draft boats.

On a calm day the sandy flats adjacent to the Cedar Island Ferry can hold a variety of game fish, including reds, stripers, flounder, and sea trout.

October is one of the most magical months to fish here, especially for redfish and specks. If you want to target tarpon, a knowledgeable guide is your best bet, as these fish are difficult to catch on a fly and you must hit the timing just right.

The bulkhead near the Ocracoke Ferry dock is a good place to probe for sea trout.

Cedar Island is a sparsely populated and quaint fishing village.

A collection of some prime saltwater fly patterns with three Epoxy Shrimp at left, a couple of Clouser Minnows middle right, several Curlybuggers top right, and diving muddlers lower right. Courtesy of Capt. Rob Modys.

Types of Fish
There is a nice variety that includes redfish, bluefish, speckled trout, Spanish mackerel, flounder, black drum, and tarpon.

Equipment to Use
Rods: 6- to 9-weight rods, 9 to 9½ feet in length.
Reels: Mechanical and large-arbor reels.
Lines: Intermediate floating line.
Leaders: 0x to 2x leaders, 9 feet in length (wire leaders should be used for bluefish).
Wading: Anglers can use chest waders but be advised that marshy areas can be like quicksand. Canoes, kayaks, and other shallow-draft boats are your best bet.

Flies to Use
Bend Back, sizes 1/0-2; Bruce's Crystal Shrimp, 1/0; Chocklett's Gummy Minnow, 2/0-2; Clouser Minnow, 2/0-2; Cowen's Baitfish, 1/0; DuBiel's Finesse Fly, 2-4; DuBiel's Lil'Hadden, 1/0-2; DuBiel's Red-Ducer, 1/0-2; Lefty's Deceiver, 2/0-2; Lefty's Half & Half, 3/0-1/0; Popovics's Surf Candy, 1/0; Tommy's Crease Fly, 1/0-2; Tommy's Eel Fly, 2/0-1/0; Trow's Minnow, 3/0-6; Walt's Saltwater Popper, 1/0-2; Wirt's Redfish Rattler, 2/0-2; Wirt's Shark Fly, 3/0.

When to Fish
Spring and fall are best. When the water warms in early summer, you can expect to find tarpon.

Season & Limits
Open year-round. The harvest and regulations depend on the species. Check the North Carolina Division of Marine Fisheries website (see address below) to find the slot limits.

Nearby Fly Fishing
You can take the ferry to the Outer Banks, Core Banks, or head south to the Morehead City area.

Accommodations & Services
Morehead City is about 45 minutes away.

Helpful Web Sites
www.ncwildlife.org/Regulations
www.ncfisheries.net
www.cedarcreekcampgroundandmarina.com
www.specfever.com

Rating
Cedar Island rates an 8. When the wind is down and the fish are biting, it can be incredible.

White ibis are frequent visitors to the salt-marsh environment of Cedar Island and the wildlife refuge.

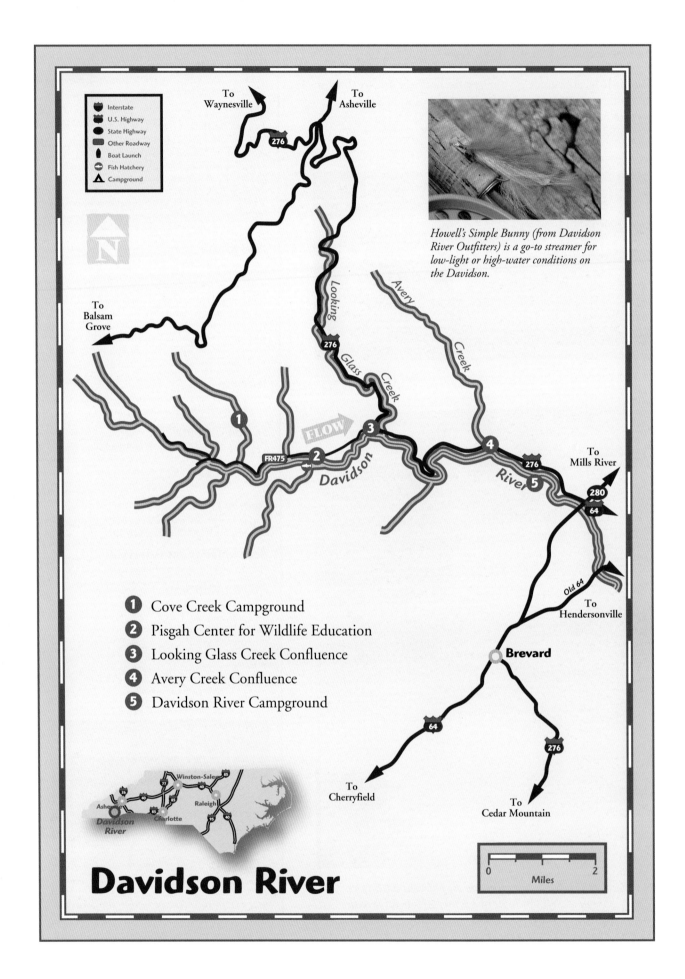

Legend:
- Interstate
- U.S. Highway
- State Highway
- Other Roadway
- Boat Launch
- Fish Hatchery
- Campground

N

To Waynesville

To Asheville

276

To Balsam Grove

Looking Glass Creek

Avery Creek

Howell's Simple Bunny (from Davidson River Outfitters) is a go-to streamer for low-light or high-water conditions on the Davidson.

276

FLOW

1

FR475

2

3

Davidson

River

4

276

5

280

64

To Mills River

Old 64

To Hendersonville

Brevard

64

276

To Cherryfield

To Cedar Mountain

1 Cove Creek Campground
2 Pisgah Center for Wildlife Education
3 Looking Glass Creek Confluence
4 Avery Creek Confluence
5 Davidson River Campground

Winston-Salem

Asheville

Davidson River

Charlotte

Raleigh

0 Miles 2

Davidson River

Davidson River

"Our tradition is that of the first man who sneaked away to the creek when the tribe did not really need fish."
— Roderick Haig-Brown, from *A River Never Sleeps*

Just west of the North Mills River is one of the most recognized and accessible trout streams in North Carolina. The Davidson River is a medium-size mountain stream that flows into the Pigeon River near the town of Brevard. I like to say the Davidson is home to "brown" university where the trout have PhDs. These fish grow large and have seen just about any fly you can imagine. Most of the water here is catch-and-release, fly-fishing only.

Stream of Consciousness

So it was the first time that I explored the Davidson. After a hearty camp breakfast, I found my little niche a few clicks below the fish hatchery and began to make some upstream casts. I was gung ho and well outfitted (or so I thought), with lots of recommended flies and looked forward to exploring this most-lauded and technical of streams. But then, I experienced a debilitating wardrobe malfunction. One of my wading boots had literally fallen apart.

Walker Parrott attempts to select the perfect fly to fool a savvy trout on the Davidson.

Tight loops and great presentation.

The Davidson River in early April, near the place where the author lost his sole.

Fortunately I was able to salvage the felt and limped back toward the Pisgah Forest Campground. Passing a married couple also there to fly fish, I explained. "I lost my sole in the river," holding up the pathetic evidence. We all had a good laugh. Later they stopped by to speak with my fishing buddy and me. They were camping in an RV, and because we were in a tent, they referred to us as "people of the cloth." They also offered some parachute cord for repairs. Fortunately I had some duct tape to help me muddle through, and I was able to resume my quest to crack the code of the Davidson River's ultra-finicky fish.

Hurry Up and Wait

This is one of Trout Unlimited's *100 Best Trout Streams*. It is a place that I personally try to avoid on weekends because it is so popular. If you cannot fish on a weekday, employ a guide for the three-mile private-water stretch of Davidson River Outfitters.

It is well known that the water level is often low on the Davidson. It is also usually quite clear. These are reasons why it is considered so technical. "Small midge imitations fished on a long 6X or 7X leader work well," says Walker Parrot. He ought to know, as he is an experienced guide with Davidson River Outfitters. These are his home waters. After some good rain, when the river level is up, he recommends using streamer patterns such as Howell's Simple Bunny or an all-around favorite known as the Sheep Fly.

The Pisgah Forest Cradle of Forestry Center and Fish Hatchery are well worth a visit. Just below the hatchery are some of the best waters to fish for large trout. The mid-section of the Davidson, from Avery Creek to the fish hatchery, is catch-and-release fly-fishing-only. Above the hatchery is a scenic gorge that may offer some semblance of solitude and the occasional large fish. The upper section is also catch-and-release. Avery and Looking Glass creeks are tributaries managed under the Wild Trout Regulations of the state wildlife commission. The hatchery-supported section of the Davidson starts at Avery Creek and runs through the Davidson River Campground until it reaches private water near Highways NC 276/64. These waters are well signed.

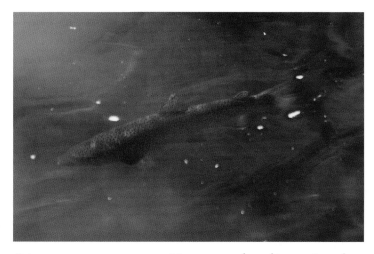

It is not uncommon to see cruising trout such as this one, in a slow-moving deep-water stretch of the Davidson River.

Types of Fish
The usual suspects include rainbow, brown, and brook trout.

Known Hatches
Baetis, Black Caddis, Black Stonefly, Blue Quill, Blue-Winged Olive, Cream Midge, Gray Caddis, Gray Fox, Green Drake, Hendrickson, Isonychia, Light Cahill, March Brown, midge, Quill Gordon, Giant Stonefly, terrestrials, Yellow Midge, Yellow Stonefly.

Equipment to Use
Rods: 4- and 5-weight, 8 to 9 feet in length
Reels: Standard.
Lines: Floating to match rod length.
Leaders: 5x to 7x, 9 through 14 feet in length.

Flies to Use
Drys: Adams, sizes 16-18; Black Beetle, 14-16; Blue Dun Thorax, 18-22; Blue-Winged Olive Parachute, 14-20; Blue Quill, 14-18; Cahill, 14-20; Coffin Fly, 14-18; Dave's Hopper, 12-14; Elk-Hair Caddis, 16-18; Flying Ant, 12-18; Griffith's Glo Bug, 14-18; Gnat, 20; Gray Midge, 18-22; Hendrickson, 14-18; Humpy, 16-18; Inchworm, 14-18; Irresistible, 14-18; Little Yellow Sally, 14-20; March Brown, 16-18; Mosquito, 14-18; Quill Gordon, 12-20; Royal Coachman, 14-18; Royal Wulff, 14-18; Stimulator, 12-18; Thunderhead, 12-16; Yellow Hammer, 10-14.

Nymphs & Streamers: Brassie, sizes 14-18; Beadhead Pheasant Tail Nymph, 16-18; Beadhead Gold-Ribbed Hare's Ear Nymph, 14-16; Bullethead Grasshopper, 10; Copper John, 14-18; Damsel, 14-16; Flashback Hare's Ear Nymph, 14-18; Gray Ghost, 8-12; Little Prince Nymph, 16-18; March Brown Nymph, 16-18; Mickey Finn, 8-10; Muddler Minnow, 6-10; Pat's Nymph, 18-24; San Juan Worm, 14-16; Scud, 12-18; Sculpin, 6-8; Stone Nymph, 6-10; Woolly Bugger, 6-10.

When to Fish
Fall and spring are the best times to fish here.

Season and Limits
The latest North Carolina Wildife Resources Commission regulations are posted on the waters, at the campground, or at nearby ranger headquarters

Nearby Fly Fishing
The area surrounding Brevard is a hotbed for fly fishing. Other rivers include the North and South Mills and the French Broad.

Accommodations and Services
The Pisgah Forest Campground and the town of Brevard are outstanding resources. Davidson River Outfitters is especially convenient.

Helpful Websites
www.davidsonflyfishing.com

Rating
Calling this a challenging stream is an understatement. The Davidson River has large finicky fish and an abundance of anglers. I rate it an 8 overall.

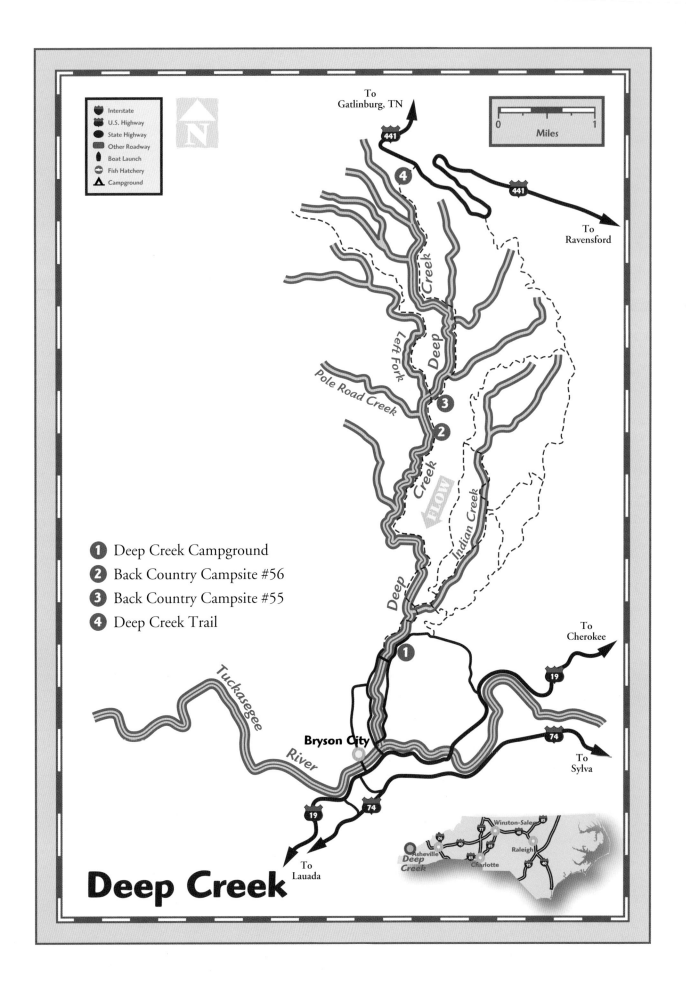

Interstate
U.S. Highway
State Highway
Other Roadway
Boat Launch
Fish Hatchery
Campground

N

To
Gatlinburg, TN

441

4

To
Ravensford

441

Creek

Left Fork

Deep

Pole Road Creek

3

2

Creek

FLOW

Indian Creek

❶ Deep Creek Campground
❷ Back Country Campsite #56
❸ Back Country Campsite #55
❹ Deep Creek Trail

Deep

1

To
Cherokee

19

Tuckasegee

74

To
Sylva

River

Bryson City

19

74

To
Lauada

Winston-Salem

77

Asheville
Deep
Creek

Charlotte

Raleigh

Deep Creek

Deep Creek

This Great Smoky Mountains National Park paradise is an hour west of Asheville and is only a stone's throw north of the charming mountain town of Bryson City. Deep Creek has its headwaters in Newfound Gap and meanders fifteen miles southward into the Tuckasegee River. The campground, a former Civilian Conservation Corps Camp, is an ideal place to start and is easy to locate, as there are plenty of signs in town.

The stream is fairly large as Smoky Mountain streams go. Emerald pools provide cover for cunning brown trout. Riffles and runs provide prime habitat for rainbows. A picnic area, ample parking, and three magnificent waterfalls make Deep Creek a popular destination for the whole family.

Fly fishers will note that *tubers* (vacationers riding inner tubes) are often found floating through the runs near the expansive park campground on warm days. A fishing buddy of mine in Oregon used to call them "splash and gigglers." During the summer months, anglers often make a beeline for the tube cut-off point a mile or so upstream of the campground area at the confluence with Indian Creek. Access beyond the parking area is all on foot along the Deep Creek Trail. Above Indian Creek, fishing conditions improve. For decades, Deep Creek has been well known for its brown trout although there is a good population of rainbows as well as brookies up near the headwaters. The trail becomes more

Types of Fish

Deep Creek is known for its wary browns but also has a good population of rainbows and brook trout as the elevation increases.

Known Hatches

Blue Quill, Blue-Winged Olive, Brown Dun, Brown Caddis, Brown Drake, Cream Caddis, Cream Cahills, Golden Stones, Giant Stoneflies, Gray Fox, Green Drake, Green Rock Worm, Green Sedge, Hendrickson, Light Cahill, Little Black Winter Stones, Little Brown Stones, March Browns, midges, Olive Caddis, Quill Gordon, Short-horned Sedge, Sulphurs, terrestrials, Tricos, Yellow Sallies, Willowflies.

Equipment to Use

Rods: 3- to 5-weight, 7½ to 9 feet in length.
Reels: Standard mechanical.
Lines: Weight-forward floating, matched to rod.
Leaders: 4x to 6x leaders, 9 feet in length.
Wading: Chest waders recommended.

Flies to Use

Drys: Adams, sizes 12-18; Black Beetle, 14-16; Blue Dun Thorax, 18-22; Blue-Winged Olive Parachute, 14-20; Blue Quill, 14-18; Cahill, 14-20; Coffin Fly, 14-18;

Continued

Deep Creek Trail was built in the 1930s by the Civilian Conservation Corps. The main campground is across the river and behind the trees.

Tom's Branch Falls is one of three scenic waterfalls on Deep Creek.

primitive and challenging as the elevation increases. Trillium, galax, and crested dwarf iris are among the wildflowers as well as thickets of rhododendron, mountain laurel, and flame azalea. Access to the stream can be difficult. Some of the better access points are near the Backcountry Campsites 53–60. Left Fork Deep Creek and Pole Road Creek are two fishable tributaries near Backcountry Campsites 55 and 56. If you plan on backpacking in, make plans to register at the park office ahead of time. The main campground is open from March through November and is $14–$23 per night. Another option for exploring the stream and the smaller brook-trout tributaries would be to pick up the arduous Deep Creek Trail from U.S. Highway 441 (Newfound Gap Road), closer to the headwaters.

The author nymphs a run at dusk on Deep Creek. Photo by Elizabeth Larson.

The confluence of Indian Creek (foreground) with Deep Creek in early April.

Flies to Use (continued)

Dave's Hopper, 12-14; Elk-Hair Caddis, 16-18; Flying Ant, 12-18; Griffith's Glo Bug, 14-18; Gnat, 20; Gray Midge, 18-22; Hendrickson, 14-18; Humpy, 16-18; Inchworm, 14-18; Irresistible, 14-18; Little Yellow Sally, 14-20; March Brown, 16-18; Mosquito, 14-18; Quill Gordon, 12-20; Royal Coachman, 14-18; Royal Wulff, 14-18; Stimulator, 12-18; Thunderhead, 12-16; Yellow Hammer, 10-14; Yellow Palmer, 12-14.

Nymph & Streamers: Brassie, sizes 14-18; Beadhead Pheasant Tail, 16-18; Beadhead Gold Ribbed Hare's Ear, 14-16; Bullethead Grasshopper, 10; Copper John, 14-18; Damsel, 14-16; Flashback Hare's Ear, 14-18; Gray Ghost, 8-12; Little Prince Nymph, 16-18; March Brown Nymph, 16-18; Mickey Finn, 8-10; Muddler Minnow, 6-10; Pat's Nymph, 18-24; San Juan Worm, 14-16; Scud, 12-18; Sculpin, 6-8; Stone Nymph, 6-10; Wickham's Nymph, 12-16; Wilkins's C.K. Emerger, 16-18; Woolly Bugger, 6-10; Y2K, 12-14; Zonker, 4-10; Zug Bug, 12-16.

When to Fish

March through early May and September through November are good months but watch the forecast for snow late in the season

Season and Limits

Open year-round. Single hook. See current regulations. Stop by park office to find out which tributaries are open.

Nearby Fly Fishing

Noland Creek, the Tuckasegee, or even the Oconaluftee are good options from here. The so-called "Road to Nowhere" on the north shore of Fontana Lake is a fascinating trail to explore.

Accomodations and Services

Bryson City is a good bet for all your angling and supply needs.

Rating

Deep Creek rates a solid 8.

Stoneflies provide food for trout. Yellow is a good choice for many Smoky Mountain fly patterns.

North Carolina's Piedmont has thousands of farm ponds in all shapes and sizes.

Farm Ponds

An Old Pond
old pond…
a frog leaps in
water's sound
 —Matsuo Basho

Big bass often attack big dragonflies.

Bullfrogs are popular bass fodder and can be imitated with various sliders or popper patterns.

Just a stone's throw or a couple of long casts from my rustic abode is a quaint little tree-shrouded farm pond. Maybe I should christen my place Castaway Cabin. It is my version of Walden Pond. Although I do not live as spartan a lifestyle as Henry David Thoreau did, I certainly like to keep things simple. Fly fishing a farm pond gets you back to basics. It is an ideal place to teach youngsters the basics or to test equipment, especially if there is ample room for a backcast. North Carolina is divided into three geographic sections: the Blue Ridge Mountains, the Piedmont, and the Coastal Plain. I live in the Piedmont, derived from the French, meaning "foothills." There are no natural lakes around here, just man-made reservoirs. The only natural lakes in the state are in the Coastal Plain and include the pocosin or swamp lakes. There are however, 16,000 farm ponds in the state.

The author has a strike on Lake Cabernet (really a vineyard pond) at the Grove Winery in northeast Guilford County. Photo by Elizabeth Larson.

Many are posted with no trespassing signs. It is strongly advised to politely seek permission from the landowner before ever attempting to catch and release fish on private property unless you want an escort from Smith & Wesson.

Farm ponds in North Carolina, as well as other states, are ideal to probe with a fly rod because these ponds often receive little pressure, and they usually hold aggressive largemouth bass, bluegills, crappie, carp, or even catfish. In addition, the smaller the pond is, the easier it is to find the fish. I think my pond is fairly typical. There is an abundance of frogs, tadpoles, damselflies, and dragonflies that bass can fatten up on. Herons, a kingfisher, and a pair of wood ducks have often been observed on the pond. The squirrels, rabbits, and deer quench their thirst along with seldom-detected nocturnal visitors.

Ponds that are densely vegetated require special tactics. Early one morning I ventured out to the edge of my pond. There was not much room to even roll cast, so I employed the famed bow and arrow technique to launch a floating frog popper. The instant it hit the surface it was hammered with a splashy strike from a feisty bass. On bigger ponds I have even been known to use my float tube as a useful way to cast to remote areas. My only concern is that one of those large truck-tire sized snapping turtles might mistake my fin for breakfast. On the biggest ponds, a canoe or small skiff works just fine. Shadowy areas, logs, docks, cattail, lily-pad edges, and tree-limb overhangs are all prime places to cast.

Bluegill are often a prevalent species in farm ponds.

Types of Fish
Largemouth bass, crappie, bluegill, sunfish, catfish, and carp are the predominant species.

Known Bait
Crayfish, minnows, small fry, frogs, tadpoles, dragon- and damselflies, and dragon- and damselfly nymphs are found in most farm ponds.

Equipment to Use
Rods: 4- to 8-weight rods can cover most situations.
Reels: Standard mechanical.
Lines: Floating weight-forward or double-taper to match rod weight.
Leaders: 9- to 15-foot leaders tapered to 2x to 4x.
Wading: Watch out for mucky, hidden holes if using waders. I prefer a float tube or small boat if possible.

Flies to Use
If you are after trophy bass use bigger hooks. Trout flies work well for panfish.

Surface: Braided Butt Damsel, sizes 6-8; DP Popper, 2-6; DP Slider, 4-6; Dave's Cricket, 4-6; Dave's Hopper, 2-6; Foam Damsel, 6-12; Walt's Frog Slider, 2-6; Whitlock's Deer-Hair Popper, 4-6; Wilkins's Fire Tiger; 4-6.

Subsurface: Black Fur Ant, sizes 6-12; Carter's Rubber-Legged Dragon, 2-6; Chocklett's Gummy Minnow, 2-6; Clouser Crayfish, 2-6; Conehead Bugger, 4-8; Chuck's Claw-Dad, Brown, 4-6; Clouser Deep Minnow, 4-6; Muddler Minnow, 2-8; Woolly Bugger, 2-12; Zonker, Olive, 4-8.

When to Fish
Spring and fall are usually the best seasons. Early mornings and evenings are ideal for topwater action.

Seasons & Limits
Most fly fishers practice catch and release, but the parameters of farm-pond fishing are primarily up to the land owner.

Rating
Each and every pond is unique, as is the experience. Overall, based on my experience, I would rate them an 8.

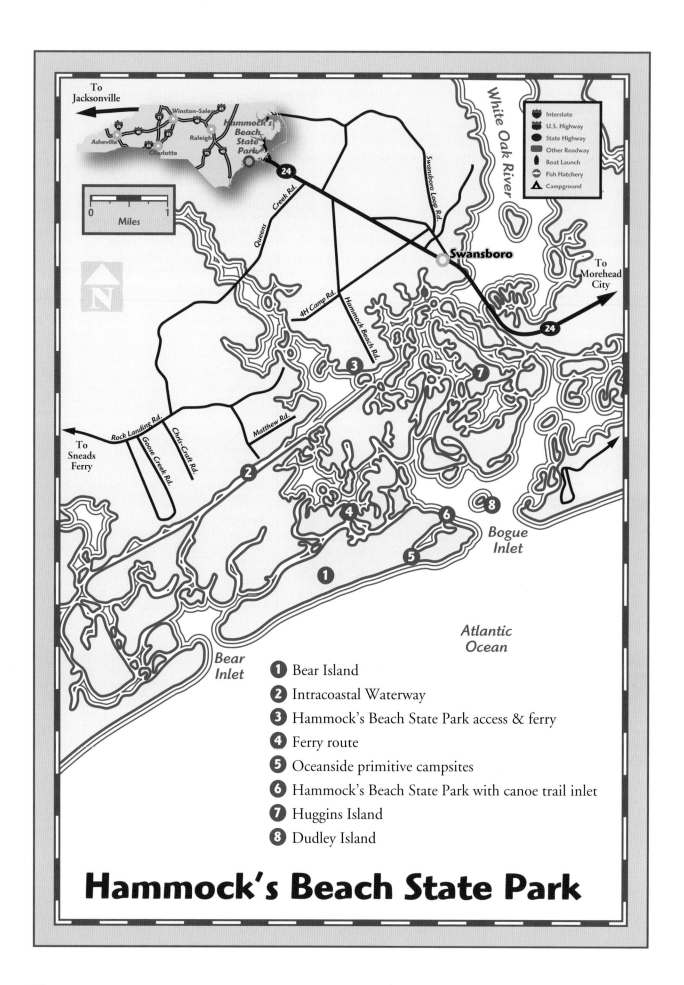

1 Bear Island
2 Intracoastal Waterway
3 Hammock's Beach State Park access & ferry
4 Ferry route
5 Oceanside primitive campsites
6 Hammock's Beach State Park with canoe trail inlet
7 Huggins Island
8 Dudley Island

Hammock's Beach State Park

Hammock's Beach State Park

Chris Tryon of Wrightsville Beach examines a selection of saltwater flies.

Sometimes it seems like a good idea to just get into a kayak and paddle. A place like Hammock's Beach State Park is ideal for those folks who enjoy the wonders of the salt marsh. My problem, or perhaps it is a blessing, is that I can only be out there so long before I get the itch to wet a fly and see what is biting. Hammock's Beach State Park is located just south of Emerald Isle and Bogue Inlet. Most of the park is on 892-acre Bear Island, a 3½-mile-long barrier island that is less than a mile wide. Dominated by large sand dunes and an old maritime forest, this place can be reached only by ferry or private boat.

Originally known as "bare island," a misspelling on an early map converted the name to "Bear." No bruins have ever been reported here, although deer and smaller mammals such as raccoons and foxes have been sighted. A kayak trail marked by buoys meanders through salt-marsh flats to a small inlet with 14 primitive campsites. There is also a ferry that takes a different route. I found the camping experience challenging but worthwhile. Desert-like conditions put a premium on shade, water, and ice. There is a bathhouse on

The author probes the waters along an edge of Bear Island. Spring and fall are the best times to fish here.

This is a view of Bear Island from the buoy-marked kayak trail. The edge of the salt marsh is a good place to troll or cast for reds, blues, or sea trout.

the island, but you need to bring your own drinking water, bug spray, sun block, and shade.

Getting to Bear Island can be tricky. If you are paddling, the best way is to time the tidal current, ride the outgoing flow at high tide, and return to the mainland in Swansboro with the incoming tide. If you plan to camp, travel light, as too much gear can weigh you down and get you stuck on the numerous sandbars. The last time I went, conditions were so calm that I was able to stand up in my flat-bottom canoe and pole my way through some of the shallows. There is plenty of interesting water to explore around the island. An intermediate sinking-tip line works well for most species. Structure such as oyster bars, depth changes, and marsh edges and channels are good places to cast. For a boat against the tide, an anchor is a good idea. One of my favorite techniques is to slow drift when the winds and tides are favorable. Often poppers and sliders can be used on frenzied bluefish that are chasing baitfish. Sometimes, early-morning specs or shallow tailing reds will rise to the occasion. I recommend a stout fluorocarbon tippet for toothy predators, even wire when you're going deep. There are a few places around Bear Island where the sand is firm enough to wade. If you do, remember the "stingray shuffle," which is a slide step that will help you scare off a ray before you step on one and get stung.

One night at Bear Island, I left camp to explore the ocean beach. In the distance I observed some small red glowing orbs. The lights were not Martians but probably park rangers checking on sea turtle nests. Campers on Bear Island are instructed not to use white lights on the beach so as not to discourage the 150- to 300-pound female loggerhead sea turtles from coming ashore and nesting in the dunes from mid-May through August.

Another island of interest within the park is Huggins Island to the east. At 225 acres, Huggins is smaller than Bear Island, and it is visible from Swansboro. Now covered with trees and thickets, Huggins has a fascinating history. The Tuscarora Indians once inhabited the area, and during the Civil War it was used as a Confederate artillery battery. Today, it is a natural sanctuary deemed a Globally Rare and Significant Area.

Chris Tryon stalking redfish in the inland waterways of coastal North Carolina.

My campsite on Bear Island. The inlet makes a good harbor for small boats.

Types of Fish
Bluefish, red drum, black drum, flounder, speckled trout, gray trout, ladyfish, croaker, Spanish mackerel, small cobia, and maybe even false albacore.

Known Baitfish
Shrimp, menhaden, mullet, crabs, squid, and other small baitfish.

Equipment to Use
Rods: 6- to 9-weight rods, 9 to 10 feet in length.
Reels: Mechanical and large-arbor reels.
Lines: Intermediate floating line, 10- to 15-foot sinking-tip lines for sea trout.
Leaders: 0x to 2x leaders, 9 feet in length (wire leaders should be used for bluefish). Use shorter, 2- to 4-foot leaders with sinking lines for flounder and sea trout.
Wading: Anglers can use chest waders as well as canoes, kayaks, or other shallow-draft boats.

Flies to Use
Bend Back, sizes 1/0-2; Bruce's Crystal Shrimp, 1/0; Clouser Minnow, 2/0-4; DuBiel's Finesse Fly, 2 and 4; DuBiel's Lil'Hadden, 1/0-2; DuBiel's Red-Ducer, 1/0-2; Lefty's Deceiver, 2/0-2; Lefty's Half & Half, 2/0-2; Popovics's Surf Candy, 1/0; Tommy's Crease Fly, 2/0-2; Tommy's Eel Fly, 2/0 and 1/0; Trow's Minnow, 3/0-6; Wirt's Redfish Rattler, 2/0-2.

When to Fish
Spring, late summer, and especially fall offer the most variety and best numbers of fish.

Season & Limits
Open all year. Limits and sizes depend on time of year and species.

Nearby Fly Fishing
The Intracoastal Waterway, White Oak River.

Accommodations & Services
The town of Swansboro is your best bet for motel lodging and gear.

Permits for the campsites are available from park personnel at Hammock's Beach State Park on the mainland.

Rating
This is a fun and, at times, challenging area to fish and deserving of a solid 8.

Croakers are in the drum family, which includes the red drum and speckled sea trout

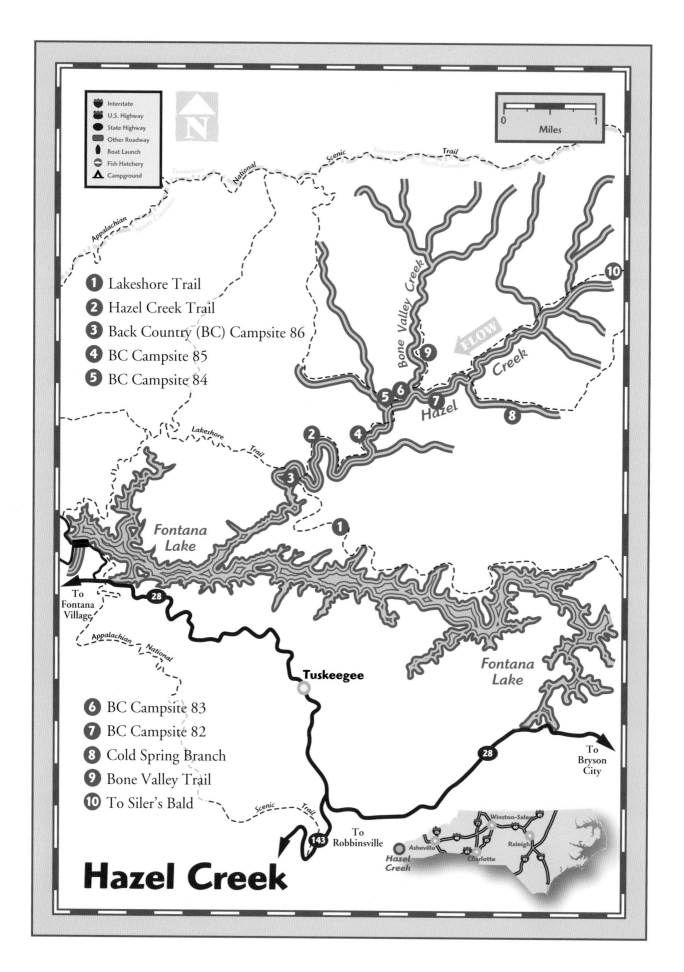

Legend

- Interstate
- U.S. Highway
- State Highway
- Other Roadway
- Boat Launch
- Fish Hatchery
- ▲ Campground

1. Lakeshore Trail
2. Hazel Creek Trail
3. Back Country (BC) Campsite 86
4. BC Campsite 85
5. BC Campsite 84

6. BC Campsite 83
7. BC Campsite 82
8. Cold Spring Branch
9. Bone Valley Trail
10. To Siler's Bald

0 — Miles — 1

Bone Valley Creek

Hazel Creek

FLOW

Tennessee Scenic Trail
North Carolina

Appalachian National Scenic Trail
North Carolina

Lakeshore Trail

Fontana Lake

To Fontana Village

28

Appalachian National

Tuskeegee

Fontana Lake

28

To Bryson City

Scenic Trail

143

To Robbinsville

Hazel Creek

Winston-Salem
Asheville
Charlotte
Raleigh
Hazel Creek

Hazel Creek

The most heralded of North Carolina trout streams, historic Hazel Creek is full of legacy, intrigue, and wild trout. The mouth of Hazel Creek is found at the northern edge of Fontana Lake in Great Smoky Mountains National Park. Anglers embark on foot or by ferry. The trip by ferry costs $50 and takes about twenty minutes for each way. Hiking in to the creek from Fontana dam would have entailed at least a 12-mile hike. The ferry ride begins at Fontana Village Resort Marina and covers nearly the length of Fontana Lake, which is surrounded by magnificent fjords reminiscent of Alaska. The ferry drops you off at the mouth of the Hazel Creek, which spills into Fontana Lake near the trailhead. Many anglers who are accustomed to fishing Hazel Creek have created ingenious devices to cart in their gear. Those funky looking strollers with bicycle tires are known as *Smoky Mountain Pushcarts*.

On my first solo sojourn to Hazel, I arrived with backpack and fly rod, and paid for the ferry at the marina. The boat snaked up into the lower reaches of the creek where massive boulders punctuate deep pocket water. Consider using streamers here as this is home to very large brown trout and even some smallmouth bass. Hiking on the lower stretches of this classic freestone stream is relatively easy.

Massive mountains mark the entrance to Hazel Creek and Great Smoky Mountains National Park.

A fly fisher stalks trout during a snowstorm on Hazel Creek. Photo by Gary Edwards.

An old railroad grade follows the contour of Hazel Creek.

There is a nice trail network that crisscrosses through the Smokies.

A pontoon ferry is a popular way to get across Fontana Lake and on to Hazel Creek.

The trail is an old railroad bed that parallels the stream. This remote area was once a well-populated community filled with people who were employed by lumber mills and mining operations before the Tennesssee Valley Authority flooded the region at the onset of World War II. Several old drying kilns remain near the trail that passes by the site of the old Ritter Saw Mill. These structures were built to dry wood used for flooring. The author Horace Kephart chronicled the everyday life of Appalachian Mountain folks, including trout fishing, while living on the headwaters of Hazel Creek near an abandoned copper mine. He wrote *Camping and Woodcraft,* first published in 1906, and another of his books, the fascinating yet somewhat controversial book titled *Our Southern Highlanders,* was published in 1913.

The Tonic of Wildness

A wealth of insect life keeps the wild-trout population in Hazel Creek healthy. There are lots of yellow stoneflies and sulfurs, but caddis are king here. Hazel Creek is also a haven for other forms of wildlife. On an April trek one year, I observed turkey, wild boar, deer, and pileated woodpeckers all on or near the riparian zone. Oh, and of course, this is bear country. One should never underestimate the mountains. Expect and be prepared for the worst weather. April snowstorms are not uncommon. While hiking up to the Bone Valley Backcountry Campsite 83, I crossed paths with some hikers who had hiked down from Clingman's Dome. They told me how they had just been waylaid by a spring snowstorm. In fact that is how Bone Valley got its name. A blizzard trapped 100 cattle back in the 1800s. Their bleached remnants are scattered about. There is a fine little cabin that still stands sentinel there today.

The first fishable branch to consider on the hike up Hazel Creek Trail is Sugar Fork, a small rainbow tributary that flows into Hazel Creek near Campsite 84, about five miles above Fontana Lake. Next is Bone Valley Creek, a half mile farther up. This popular tributary holds rainbow trout in the ten- to fourteen-inch range with some brookies in smaller prongs upstream. Take note that the Bone Valley Creek Trail is not well maintained after 1.7 miles. Continuing up Hazel Creek Trail, go past Calhoun Campsite 82 to Proctor Creek Camp 81 at the 10.5-mile mark. From here up to Hazel Creek Cascades Campsite 80, it is all steep brook-trout country.

Runs, riffles, and pools are plentiful at Hazel Creek.

Types of Fish
Wild brook, browns, and rainbows

Known Hatches
Baetis, Black Caddis, Black Stonefly, Blue Quill, Blue-Winged Olive, Cream Midge, Gray Caddis, Gray Fox, Green Drake, Hendrickson, Isonychia, Light Cahill, March Brown, midge, Quill Gordon, Giant Stonefly, terrestrials, Yellow Midge, Yellow Stonefly.

Equipment to Use
Rods: 4- to 6-weight rod, preferably four-piece for backpacking.
Reels: Standard mechanical.
Lines: Weight-forward floating, matched to rod.
Leaders: 5x to 6x.

Flies to Use
Drys: Adams, sizes 16-18; Black Beetle, 14-16; Blue Thorax Dun, 18-22; Blue-Winged Olive Parachute, 14-20; Blue Quill, 14-18; Cahill, 14-20; Coffin Fly, 14-18; Dave's Hopper, 12-14; Elk-Hair Caddis, 16-18; Flying Ant, 12-18; Griffith's Glo Bug, 14-18; Gnat, 20; Gray Midge, 18-22; Hendrickson, 14-18; Humpy, 16-18; Inchworm, 14-18; Irresistible, 14-18; Little Yellow Sally, 14-20; March Brown, 16-18; Mosquito, 14-18; Quill Gordon, 12-20; Royal Coachman, 14-18; Royal Wulff, 14-18; Stimulator, 12-18; Thunderhead, 12-16; Yellow Hammer, 10-14.

Nymphs & Streamers: Brassie, sizes 14-18; Beadhead Pheasant Tail, 16-18; Beadhead Gold-Ribbed Hare's Ear, 14-16; Bullethead Grasshopper, 10; Copper John, 14-18; Damsel, 14-16; Flashback Hare's Ear, 14-18; Gray Ghost, 8-12; Little Prince Nymph, 14-18; March Brown Nymph, 16-18; Mickey Finn, 8-10; Muddler Minnow, 6-10; Pat's Nymph, 18-24; San Juan Worm, 14-16; Scud, 12-18; Sculpin, 6-8; Stone Nymph, 6-10; Woolly Bugger, 6-10.

When to Fish
This stream is open year-round but is not recommended in winter or when winter-like conditions occur in the early spring and fall.

Season & Limits
Open year-round. Like most fly fishers, we encourage catch and release.

Nearby Fly Fishing
Eagle Creek is a five-mile hike west from the confluence of Hazel Creek and the Fontana Lake Trail. Eagle Creek is similar to Hazel Creek but gets less pressure.

Accommodation & Services
Bryson City, Cherokee, and Fontana Village are close to the southern edge of Fontana Lake and have basic supplies and some fly shops.

Fontana Marina, (828) 498-2211, extension 2129, or 1-800-849-2258, ask for the marina. The ferry costs $25 one way, $50 round trip. If you want to use your own boat, another access point is the Cable Cove Campground public boat ramp at the end of Cable Cove Road (N.C. Highway 28).

Rating
This is the most popular stream in the Smokies and deserving of a solid 9.

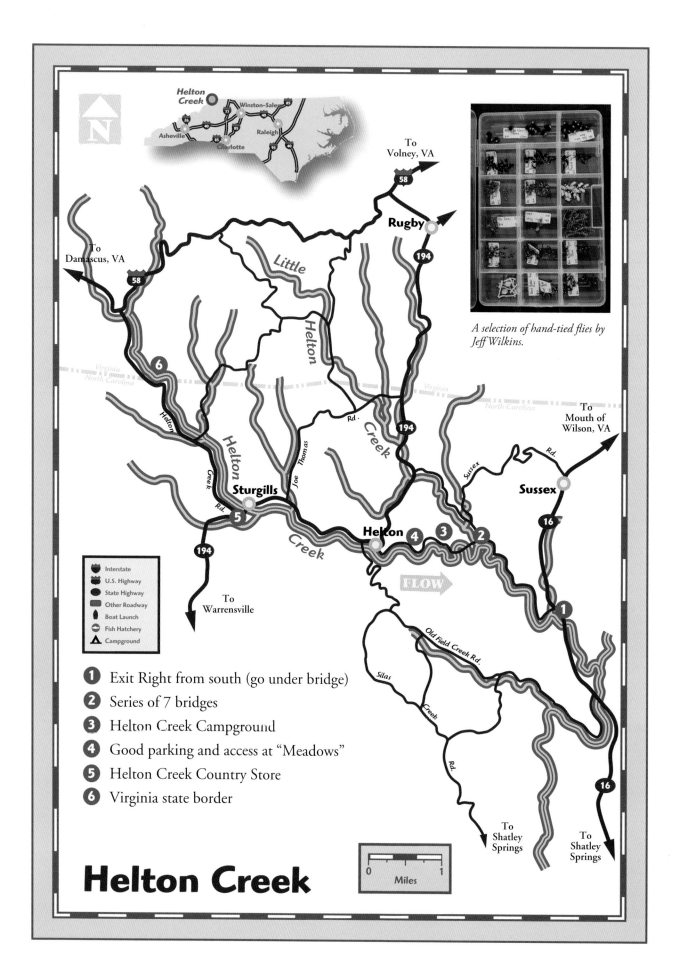

A selection of hand-tied flies by Jeff Wilkins.

Legend:
- Interstate
- U.S. Highway
- State Highway
- Other Roadway
- Boat Launch
- Fish Hatchery
- Campground

1. Exit Right from south (go under bridge)
2. Series of 7 bridges
3. Helton Creek Campground
4. Good parking and access at "Meadows"
5. Helton Creek Country Store
6. Virginia state border

Helton Creek

0   1
Miles

Helton Creek

Jeff Wilkins shows off his trophy, landed using a 3-weight rod.

The main stem of Helton Creek in northern Ashe County is a top-notch, cold-weather, delayed-harvest trout destination in the Blue Ridge Mountains. It is a tributary to the North Fork of the New River. A winter trip here feels and looks like something out of a postcard because this is Christmas tree country. Fraser firs are a huge agribusiness and make Ashe County one of the biggest Christmas tree–producing counties in the nation. With the borders of Virginia to the north and Tennessee to the west, this mountain region is more isolated and less cluttered than most of the other Carolina "ski mountain" destinations. The terrain is open farmland mixed with hardwoods and good access to the creek.

The Helton Creek area was once the sacred hunting ground of the Shawnee, Creek, and Cherokee people before Europeans arrived in the 1700s. Early frontiersmen included namesake David Helton and the American legend Daniel Boone. Guide and friend Jeff Wilkins took me here and easily convinced me that this was a special place. With his knowledge of the stream and some of his finely crafted flies, I managed to catch an impressive mix of

A monster rainbow explodes on a fly in a Helton Creek pool.

Jeff Wilkins works his way upstream on Helton Creek.

brookies, browns, and rainbows. Then I coaxed my patient guide to try *his* luck, or more precisely, expertise. He handled that little 3-weight fly rod like a magician. Somehow he was able to sniff out and fool some of the biggest 'bows I had ever seen anywhere, especially on a Southern mountain stream. The trophy of the day was a 28-inch rainbow behemoth that tipped the scale at 8 pounds.

One of my favorite techniques to use on this stream is a double-fly rig: a standard nymph, followed several inches down—depending on the depth of the water—by a smaller pupa or emerger as the trailing fly. Sometimes a dry fly such as a yellow Stimulator or grasshopper will be used as an indicator on the top with a wet fly, nymph or San Juan worm below. This stream is popular so don't hesitate to try something new including multi-fly rigs. Stealth is also emphasized as the water is often very low and clear.

From N.C. Highway 421 take 194 north to Highway 16, go left on 16 and cross the New River. You can catch and release all the way up to the Virginia border.

Detail of a 28-inch rainbow trout.

Helton Creek often runs low and clear during the late fall and winter months.

Types of Fish
Brook trout, browns, and rainbows.

Known Hatches
Baetis, Black Caddis, Black Stonefly, Blue Quill, Blue-Winged Olive, Cream Midge, Gray Caddis, Gray Fox, Green Drake, Hendrickson, Isonychia, Light Cahill, March Brown, midge, Quill Gordon, Giant Stonefly, terrestrials, Yellow Midge, Yellow Stonefly,

Equipment to Use
Rods: 8 foot or less, 3- to 5-weight rod.
Reels: Standard mechanical.
Lines: Weight-forward floating, matched to rod.
Leaders: 4x to 6x leaders, 9 feet long.
Wading: Hip waders can be used, but chest waders are recommended for the deeper holes.

Flies to Use
Drys: Adams, sizes 16-22; Black Beetle, 14-16; Blue-Winged Olive Parachute, 14-20; Blue Quill, 14-18; Cahill, 14-20; Coffin Fly, 14-18; Dave's Hopper, 12-14; Elk-Hair Caddis, 16-18; Flying Ant, 12-18; Glo Bug, 14-18; Griffith's Gnat, 20; Hendrickson, 14-18; Humpy, 16-18; Inchworm, 14-18; Irresistible, 14-18; Little Yellow Sally, 14-20; March Brown, 16-18; Mosquito, 14-18; Olive Midge, 18-24; Quill Gordon, 12-20; Royal Coachman, 14-18; Royal Wulff, 14-18; Stimulator, 12-18.

Nymphs & Streamers: Brassie, sizes 14-18; Beadhead Pheasant Tail, 16-18; Beadhead Gold-Ribbed Hare's Ear, 14-16; Beadhead Prince Nymph, 14-18; Black Stonefly Nymph, size 18; Copper John, 14-18; Damsel, 14-16; Flashback Hare's Ear, 14-18; Gray Midge, 18-24; Little Prince Nymph, 16-18; March Brown Nymph, 16-18; Mickey Finn, 8-10; Muddler Minnow, 6-10; Pat's Nymph, 18-24; San Juan Worm, 14-16; Scud, 12-18; Sculpin, 6-8; Stone Nymph, 6-10; Woolly Bugger, 6-10; Y2K, size 10.

When to Fish
Fall, from October through winter, and early spring are all good times to fish Helton Creek.

Season & Limits
As of this writing, this is catch-and-release water from October 1 through June 4. Under delayed-harvest regulations, no trout can be harvested during that period. Single-hook and artificial lures may be used. No natural bait is allowed or any lure treated with taste or smell enhancements.

Nearby Fly Fishing
The New River, Big Horse Creek, Big Laurel Creek, and Buffalo Creek are your closest alternatives.

Accommodations & Services
The town of Jefferson, southwest of Helton Creek, has a variety of services and places to stay. Visit the Ashe County Visitor's guide at www.ashechamber.com for full details.

Rating
This is a fine place to tangle with a good quantity and quality of trout in a serene location.

I recommend visiting on a weekday if possible. My experience here has been superb. I rate it a 9.

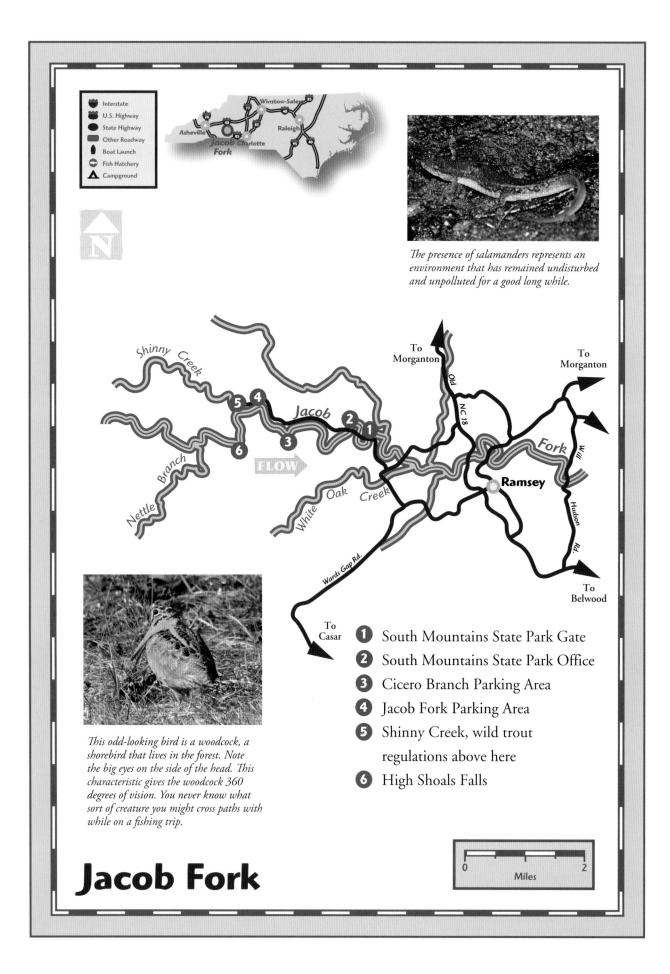

Interstate
U.S. Highway
State Highway
Other Roadway
Boat Launch
Fish Hatchery
Campground

N

The presence of salamanders represents an environment that has remained undisturbed and unpolluted for a good long while.

Shinny Creek

Jacob

Nettle Branch

FLOW

White Oak Creek

To Morganton

Old

NC 18

To Morganton

Fork

Will

Ramsey

Hudson Rd.

To Belwood

Wards Gap Rd.

To Casar

This odd-looking bird is a woodcock, a shorebird that lives in the forest. Note the big eyes on the side of the head. This characteristic gives the woodcock 360 degrees of vision. You never know what sort of creature you might cross paths with while on a fishing trip.

1 South Mountains State Park Gate
2 South Mountains State Park Office
3 Cicero Branch Parking Area
4 Jacob Fork Parking Area
5 Shinny Creek, wild trout regulations above here
6 High Shoals Falls

0   Miles   2

Jacob Fork

Jacob Fork

Where the mountains meet the Piedmont, you will find a unique and enchanting destination called *South Mountains State Park*. Only a half-hour drive from Morganton, Jacob Fork is literally a stream set apart.

The South Mountains are somewhat of a geographical anomaly, almost like a happy accident. They stand isolated from the rest of North Carolina's mountains. The crown jewel of the 18,000-acre park is the 80-foot High Shoals waterfall that plummets into a rugged canyon. For most fly fishers, the falls mark the genesis of the fishable portion of Jacob Fork Creek. Above the falls, and below, to the confluence of Shinny Creek (pronounced Shiny), this rough and tumble freestone stream is home to wild trout. From the confluence of Shinny Creek, all the way to the lower park boundary gate, this main stem is delayed-harvest water that receives periodic stockings.

Summer and weekends are the busiest times at South Mountains State Park.

There are three campgrounds that require reservations: a primitive campground for guys like me who don't mind packing

Types of Fish
Jacob Fork is known mostly for brown and rainbow trout. There are some native wild brookies above the falls.

Known Hatches
Baetis, Black Caddis, Black Stonefly, Blue Quill, Blue-Winged Olive, Cream Midge, Gray Caddis, Gray Fox, Hendrickson, Isonychia, Light Cahill, March Brown, midge, Quill Gordon, Giant Stonefly, terrestrials, Yellow Midge, Yellow Stonefly.

Equipment to Use
Rods: 3- to 4-weight rods.
Reels: Standard.
Lines: Floating to match rod.
Leaders: 9- to 10-foot tapered leaders from 5x to 7x.
Wading: Wet wading in warm weather. Hip boots are ok near the banks, but watch out for deep holes. Chest waders are best.

Flies to Use
Drys: Adams, sizes 16-18; Black Beetle, 14-16; Blue Thorax Dun, 18-22; Blue-Winged Olive Parachute, 14-20;

Continued

The falls upstream of High Shoals on the Jacob Fork.

Rough and tumble pocket water is home to wild trout just below the falls.

everything in on their backs, a family campground, and an equestrian campground. There are mountain-bike trails, bridle paths, hiking trails, and angler paths along the small but timeless Jacob Fork. It is recommended that anglers stay within park boundaries as there is mostly private land below the entrance gate.

Watch Your Step

In warm weather, watch out for pit vipers. The most common are copperheads. There are also some reclusive timber rattlers. Michael Eisch has been a park ranger at South Mountains for four years and has yet to see a bear. He knows they are out there, though he says the most interesting critter he has seen in the park was a four-legged trout predator more commonly called a mink. I told him about the out-of-season woodcock that I had seen. Usually by mid-winter, these odd-looking game birds have moved on farther south. We talked about the Jacob Fork and that made me want to get out there. Concluding my conversation with Ranger Eisch on an overcast February day, I decided to gear up and hunt for holdover trout.

Ah yes, winter on the Jacob Fork, fly rod in hand, truly the quiet sport. A few hours later, there I was, the lone angler in the park, loving life. I perched on the edge of a rock, minding my own business, working a Woolly Bugger through deep water for a cagey brown trout. The babbling brook that feeds the pool carried away my worries until a loud, shrill bark nearly shocked me out of my boots. I turned around to see a bounding mass of black fur and thought, "Bear." Instead, it was a large menacing dog—maybe some fugitive bear hound with a red collar. The beast stopped and growled. I played it cool, responding with my best reasonable and rational tone of voice. Somehow this convinced my tormentor to break the standoff, and he disappeared as quickly as he arrived. Finally I relaxed and tucked the can of pepper spray back into my vest pocket and called it a day.

To get to the park from I-40, turn south on N.C. 18. The route is well signed.

High water and full color on the Jacob Fork.

Alien life form? No, this nymph is a delectable menu item for a trout.

Flies to Use (continued)

Blue Quill, 14-18; Cahill, 14-20; Coffin Fly, 14-18; Dave's Hopper, 12-14; Elk-Hair Caddis, 16-18; Flying Ant, 12-18; Griffith's Glo Bug, 14-18; Gnat, 20; Gray Midge, 18-22; Hendrickson, 14-18; Humpy, 16-18; Inchworm, 14-18; Irresistible, 14-18; Little Yellow Sally, 14-20; March Brown, 16-18; Mosquito, 14-18; Quill Gordon, 12-20; Royal Coachman, 14-18; Royal Wulff, 14-18; Sheep Fly, 14-18; Stimulator, 12-18; Thunderhead, 12-16; Yellow Hammer, 10-14.

Nymphs & Streamers: Brassie, sizes 14-18; Beadhead Pheasant Tail Nymph, 16-18; Beadhead Gold-Ribbed Hare's Ear Nymph, 14-16; Bullethead Grasshopper, 10; Copper John, 14-18; Damsel, 14-16; Flashback Hare's Ear Nymph, 14-18; Gray Ghost, 8-12; Little Prince Nymph, 16-18; March Brown Nymph, 16-18; Mickey Finn, 8-10; Muddler Minnow, 6-10; Pat's Nymph, 18-24; San Juan Worm, 14-16; Scud, 12-18; Sculpin, 6-8; Stone Nymph, 6-10; Woolly Bugger, 6-10; Wickham's Nymph, 12-16.

When to Fish

Fall and spring offer the most bug activity but winter offers solitude, although cold weather can make the trout lethargic and elusive.

Season & Limits

Generally from October to early June, anglers cannot harvest or possess trout from the Delayed Harvest section of the Jacob Fork. From June to October, hatchery-supported regulations allow for such. Within Wild Trout Waters, the legal creel limit is four, with a minimum length of seven inches. The NCWRC is very good at posting the diamond-shaped regulatory signs on the various stream banks. If you have any other questions consult the NCWRC Regulations Digest; www.ncwildlife.org. The best rule of thumb is to practice catch and release.

Nearby Fly Fishing

Good destinations include The Henry Fork, Lake James, and Wilson Creek.

Accommodations & Services

South Mountains State Park has eleven primitive campsites plus group and backpack camping. Call 1-877-7-CAMPNC for reservations or check out this website: www.ncparks.gov.

The city of Morganton is only about eighteen miles north of the park and has a wide range of amenities.

Rating

This is a good place to teach a kid how to fly fish. It is a fine little stream that rates an 8.

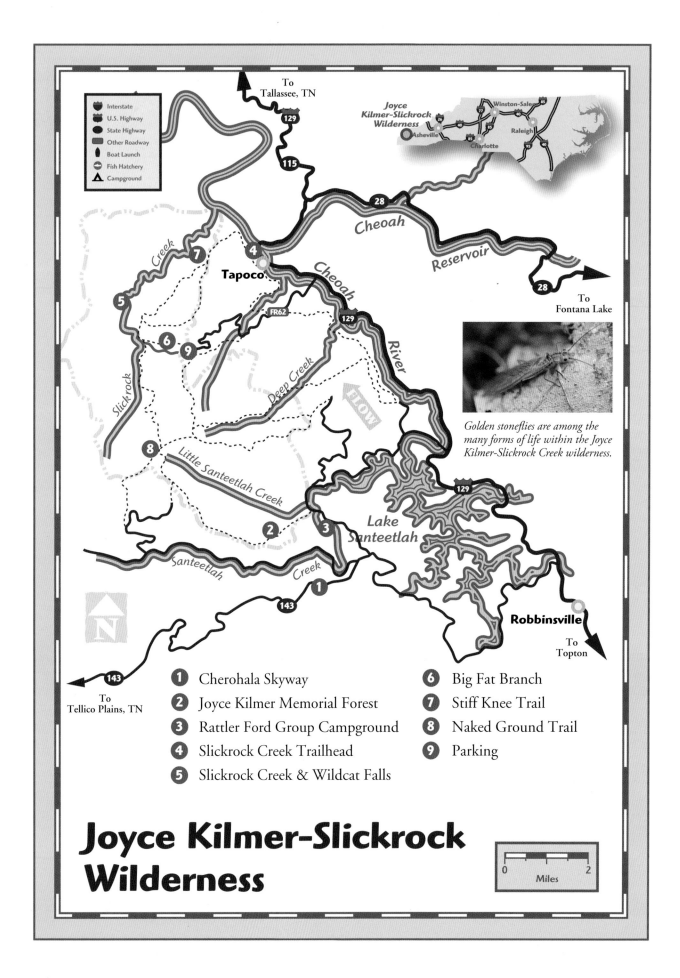

Legend:
- Interstate
- U.S. Highway
- State Highway
- Other Roadway
- Boat Launch
- Fish Hatchery
- Campground

To Tallassee, TN

Joyce Kilmer-Slickrock Wilderness

Winston-Salem

Asheville

Charlotte

Raleigh

Cheoah Reservoir

To Fontana Lake

Tapoco

Cheoah River

FR62

Slickrock Creek

Deep Creek

FLOW

Golden stoneflies are among the many forms of life within the Joyce Kilmer-Slickrock Creek wilderness.

Little Santeetlah Creek

Lake Santeetlah

Santeetlah Creek

Robbinsville

To Topton

N

To Tellico Plains, TN

① Cherohala Skyway
② Joyce Kilmer Memorial Forest
③ Rattler Ford Group Campground
④ Slickrock Creek Trailhead
⑤ Slickrock Creek & Wildcat Falls

⑥ Big Fat Branch
⑦ Stiff Knee Trail
⑧ Naked Ground Trail
⑨ Parking

Joyce Kilmer-Slickrock Wilderness

0   Miles   2

Joyce Kilmer– Slickrock Wilderness

Deep in the mountains of western North Carolina, adjacent to the Tennessee border, there is a wild and mystical place: the Joyce Kilmer Memorial Forest. The Kilmer forest is home to some of the most ancient old-growth forest in the eastern United States. A couple of fine trout streams, the Little Santeetlah and Slickrock creeks, meander through this magnificent area, which is also part of Nantahala National Forest.

There is something sacred about the shape and bearing of a huge tree with its towering canopy, massive root system, and quiet nobility. Multiply that by a choice expanse of virgin timber, and you get the enchanting environment that is the Joyce Kilmer Memorial Forest.

You may not recall Alfred Joyce Kilmer, but you probably are familiar with his well-known poem, "Trees," which begins with the famous line, "I think that I shall never see / A poem lovely as a tree." Kilmer had worked as a dictionary editor, a writer for the *New York Times,* and was an honored U.S. patriot. During World War I, he was a well-respected sergeant in the Fighting 69th Infantry Regiment. He was killed in action while volunteering on a dangerous mission in France. Thanks to the persuasion of the Veterans of Foreign Wars, the Joyce Kilmer Memorial Forest was dedicated to his memory on July 10, 1936.

Little Santeetlah Creek is shrouded by rhododendrons and is home to wild trout.

Feisty wild rainbow trout in the Little Santeetlah are opportunists and will pounce on a well-presented fly.

The author illustrates the scale of one of the towering old-growth trees.

The waters within the Joyce Kilmer Slickrock Creek
wilderness area are some of the most pristine in the state.

Little Santeetlah

When I go fishing I…want to get away from it all, for it is silence and solitude even more than it is fish that I am seeking…As for big fish, all is relative. Not every tuna is a trophy.
  —William Humphrey, from *My Moby Dick*

The Little Santeetlah is a small yet regal stream located within the Joyce Kilmer Memorial Forest that is a part of Joyce Kilmer–Slickrock Wilderness. *Santeetlah* is an Indian term for "blue waters." The Little Santeetlah flows into Santeetlah Creek and has a population of small wild trout surrounded by an impressive forest in the Poplar Cove section that includes very large virgin tulip poplars, oak, and hickory trees, some up to 450 years old. This is the kind of place that can make you feel like a wide-eyed kid, with the diversity of plant, animal, and insect life. To explore the big trees and Little Santeetlah Creek, from Robbinsville, go west on N.C. 143. Travel 12 miles to County Road 1127/1134, which also bears the names Santeetlah Road and Joyce Kilmer Road, turn right (north) and follow the signs.

Slickrock Creek

For anglers who want to get the most out of this experience, plan on backpacking. Hiking here requires good planning, sure footedness, proper gear, maps, compass skills, a fit companion, and a suitable allotment of time. A good guidebook is *Hiking Trails of the Joyce Kilmer-Slickrock and Citico Creek Wildernesses,* by Tim Homan. Slickrock Creek Trail is 13½ miles long, includes numerous creek crossings, and follows the border with Tennessee.

Sixty miles of trails crisscross the wilderness; many lead to Slickrock Creek and have names such as Naked Ground and Stiff Knee. The creek features some very nice pools and cascades including Lower Falls and Wildcat Falls. Wildcat has four tiers of cascades, and the last one pours into a pool that is known as a popular swimming hole, but I would fish it first, before splashing around.

The timber is old-growth and has fewer virgin trees than the Poplar Cove area near Little Santeetlah but still has some impressive stands. Due to its Wilderness designation, if a tree falls, it stays there. Uncleared paths can be difficult to follow. A final caveat: in late fall, be aware that bear and boar hunters frequent the area.

Slickrock Creek originates in the Unicoi Mountains, is a tributary of the Little Tennessee River, and is known for its almost exclusive population of brown trout. They were shuttled into the watershed in custom backpacks by members of the Civilian Conservation Corps. These modern-day heirlooms are said to have the most vibrant colors of any brown trout in the region.

The elusive green drake mayfly hatch in April or May is another draw for fly fishers. North Carolina has a reciprocal license agreement with Tennessee just in case you are caught fishing on the other side of the border.

The trailhead is located just off U.S. 129 near the Cheoah River on the southern side of the Cheoah Dam. Ike Branch Trail is the easiest way to begin, as it bisects the Slickrock Creek trail. The early part of the trail is of moderate difficulty and later becomes more strenuous and hard to follow. This trail can be wet due to stream crossings and, as the name implies, is slippery at times.

Types of Fish
Mostly brown trout with a few brookies in the upper stretches.

Known Hatches
Baetis, Black Caddis, Black Stonefly, Blue Quill, Blue-Winged Olive, Cream Midge, Gray Caddis, Gray Fox, Green Drake, Hendrickson, Isonychia, Light Cahill, March Brown, midge, Quill Gordon, Giant Stonefly, terrestrials, Yellow Midge, Yellow Stonefly.

Equipment to Use
Rods: 3- to 4-weight for nymphs and dry flies, 5-weight for streamers, 6 to 8½ feet in length. A 4-piece rod, with its shorter case, is convenient for hiking.
Reels: Any mechanical reel.
Lines: Floating lines to match rod weight.
Leaders: 9- to 12-foot leaders tapered to 4x through 6x.
Wading: Chest waders are recommended due to the deeper pools. Wet wading may be advantageous in the summer.

Flies to Use
Drys: Adams, sizes 16-18; Black Beetle, 14-16; Blue Thorax Dun, 18-22; Blue-Winged Olive Parachute, 14-20; Blue Quill, 14-18; Cahill, 14-20; Coffin Fly, 14-18; Dave's Hopper, 12-14; Elk-Hair Caddis, 16-18; Flying Ant, 12-18; Griffith's Glo Bug, 14-18; Gnat, 20; Gray Midge, 18-22; Hendrickson, 14-18; Humpy, 16-18; Inchworm, 14-18; Irresistible, 14-18; Little Yellow Sally, 14-20; March Brown, 16-18; Mosquito, 14-18; Quill Gordon, 12-20; Royal Coachman, 14-18; Royal Wulff, 14-18; Sheep Fly, 14-18; Stimulator, 12-18; Thunderhead, 12-16; Yellow Hammer, 10-14.

Nymphs & Streamers: Brassie, sizes 14-18; Beadhead Pheasant Tail Nymph, 16-18; Beadhead Gold-Ribbed Hare's Ear Nymph, 14-16; Bullethead Grasshopper, 10; Copper John, 14-18; Damsel, 14-16; Flashback Hare's Ear Nymph, 14-18; Gray Ghost, 8-12; Little Prince Nymph, 16-18; March Brown Nymph, 16-18; Mickey Finn, 8-10; Muddler Minnow, 6-10; Pat's Nymph; 18-24; San Juan Worm, 14-16; Scud, 12-18; Sculpin, 6-8; Stone Nymph, 6-10; Woolly Bugger, 6-10; Wickham's Nymph, 12-16.

When to Fish
Spring is good, summer is fair, and fall is excellent.

Season and Limits
Year-round fishing. Most fly fishers practice catch and release.

Nearby Fly Fishing
Santeetlah Creek, Big Snowbird Creek.

Accommodations & Services
Robbinsville is the closest town of any size.

The friendly folks at Cheoah Ranger Station (828-479-6431) in Robbinsville offer maps and information.

Helpful Websites
www.joycekilmerslickrock.com
www.ReserveUSA.com

Rating
Just the experience of being in a place like this makes the trip worthwhile; add the fly-fishing element and you have a solid 9.

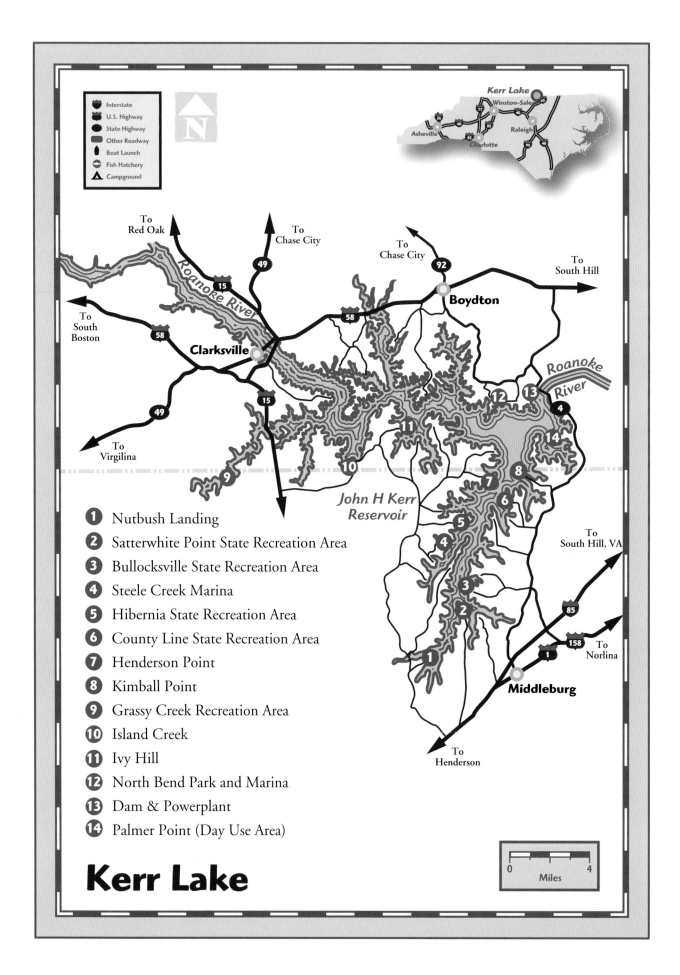

Legend

- Interstate
- U.S. Highway
- State Highway
- Other Roadway
- Boat Launch
- Fish Hatchery
- Campground

N

Kerr Lake
Winston-Salem
Asheville
Charlotte
Raleigh

To
Red Oak

To
Chase City

To
Chase City

To
South Hill

To
South
Boston

Roanoke River

49

15

58

Clarksville

58

92

Boydton

Roanoke
River

4

12

13

15

49

To
Virgilina

9

11

10

14

8

John H Kerr
Reservoir

7

6

5

4

3

2

1

To
South Hill, VA

85

158

To
Norlina

1

Middleburg

To
Henderson

1. Nutbush Landing
2. Satterwhite Point State Recreation Area
3. Bullocksville State Recreation Area
4. Steele Creek Marina
5. Hibernia State Recreation Area
6. County Line State Recreation Area
7. Henderson Point
8. Kimball Point
9. Grassy Creek Recreation Area
10. Island Creek
11. Ivy Hill
12. North Bend Park and Marina
13. Dam & Powerplant
14. Palmer Point (Day Use Area)

0   Miles   4

Kerr Lake

Kerr Lake

Jim Burchette and his friend Troy Branham were exploring a small creek on expansive Kerr Lake one cold winter day, and they grew excited when their depth finder began marking fish. Soon birds showed up to make meals of baitfish that were being pushed to the surface by foraging stripers—the bite was on. The action was rapid fire—casting and fighting and landing fish, maybe a half dozen, in just a few minutes. Then, just as quickly as it had begun, the action was over. The birds moved on, too.

The two men just sat there grinning when they heard the sound of another boat. They watched the conventional anglers troll by the mouth of the creek within earshot. Burchette overheard one of them say, "Those boys have no idea what they're doing." The two fly fishers just looked at each other and said, "That's good, let them keep thinking that!"

Jim Burchette has been fly fishing since he was 14. When I met Jim he lived in Timberlake, North Carolina, and worked at Duke University. He now lives in Tennessee. He says he works to fly fish. I met him through the Triangle Fly Fishing Club, where he had given a presentation on the art of fly fishing Kerr Lake for stripers during cold weather. His boat was an 18-foot center-console Xpress, a welded-aluminum craft powered by a

There is always the possibility of hooking one of Kerr Lake's giant cats. Photo by Troy Branham.

Jim Burchette enjoys fishing Kerr Lake in winter, and stripers such as this one are the reasons why. Photo by Troy Branham.

A sinking line is effective for probing the deep waters of Kerr Lake, home to record-size catfish. Photo by Troy Branham.

This raft of winter loons surfaced near the author's kayak. Loons are a symbol of a healthy and clean environment.

Jim Burchette displays a sizable fly-caught striper. He notes that colder temperatures often make for better fishing at Kerr Lake. Photo by Troy Branham.

four-stroke 90-horsepower Yamaha. Over several winters, he never saw another fly fisherman out there.

Some Rivers Run Through It

One of the most diverse fishing lakes in the state, Kerr Lake, officially known as John H. Kerr Reservoir but also known as Buggs Island Lake, straddles the North Carolina–Virginia border. There is good access to the lake just north of the town of Henderson, and with 900 miles of shoreline, it is one of the biggest reservoirs in the Southeast. Completed in 1952, it impounds the Roanoke River (called the Staunton River between the cities of Roanoke and Clarksville, Virginia) and provides electricity and flood control to north-central North Carolina and south-central Virginia. Anglers like it primarily for its population of largemouth bass, crappie, catfish, and stripers.

It is also known to be one of only a handful of lakes that is home to naturally reproducing striped bass. A deep lake, the average depth is said to be about 30 feet, but some areas are more than 100 feet deep. Burchette usually fishes 25 feet deep or less with a full-sinking line and always has an extra rod with a floating line rigged with a silver Crease Fly in case the stripers are near the surface. He usually fishes a two-fly rig with a small Clouser on top and a bigger Clouser on the bottom. Some of his favored color combinations include silver and white, and gold and yellow. He likes Half & Half patterns in chartreuse and white, white on white with silver Crystal Flash, or white on white with red Crystal Flash. Another go-to fly is a pink-and-chartreuse creation dubbed Tutti Frutti or Electric Chicken that he learned from Capt. Lee Parsons out of Wilmington, North Carolina.

Some of the best fishing is up near the dam where the water temperature may be a bit warmer or down in the lower creek branches. There is a reciprocal fishing license with Virginia that allows you to fish freely on both sides of the border.

According to Burchette, who enjoyed the solitude of this great cold-water fishery, there is a rule of thumb—the worse the weather, the better the striper fishing. For me, it brings to mind bone-chilling steelhead fishing in the Northwest, although he says when the water dips below 40 degrees, the bass are not so easy to catch. Burchette does not troll but watches his depth finder and keeps an eye on the sky for bird activity. He casts around riprap, points, and rocky outcrops. He says that even when you are not marking fish, they still may be there, just out of the range of the fish finder. When the wind is up he employs a drift anchor, basically a submerged snow cone to slow down the drift. He says an average Kerr striper on the fly is about 24 to 28 inches. His best was a 48 incher. He has lost fish that bent the stainless steel hooks required for big streamers. On an average day he might catch and release a half dozen. A dozen is excellent, and he has had double-digit days that surpass that.

Interstate 85 passes southeast of Kerr Lake, and there are several exits along this stretch that will put you close to the water: Exit 214 to Highway 39 heading north from Henderson; Exit 217 to Satterwhite Point; and Exit 223 to Bullocksville, County Line, and Kimball Point.

Types of Fish
Largemouth bass, striped bass, white bass, white perch, crappie, flathead catfish, channel catfish, blue catfish, bream, and primitives such as bowfin and alligator gar.

Known Hatches
Threadfin and grizzard shad and smaller fish.

Equipment to Use
Rods: 6- to 9-weight rods, 8 to 9 feet in length.
Reels: A large-arbor reel with a good disc drag will be needed for putting pressure on big fish.
Line: Floating, intermediate, and 350- to 450-grain sinking lines matched to rod weights.
Leaders: 7- to 9-foot tapered leaders from 15- to 20-pound test at the tippet for floating lines and 4- to 6-foot fluoro lines for intermediate and sinking lines.
Wading: A boat with some good horsepower is best to chase birds and find the fish. In the warmer months, kayaks or canoes can be challenging and rewarding as well.

Flies to Use
Surface: Blados's Crease Fly, sizes 1/0-2; Walt's Frog Slider, 2; Walt's Saltwater Popper, 1/0-2; Wilkins's Fire Tiger, 1/0-2.

Subsurface: #2-2/0 Chocklett's Gummy Minnow, sizes 2/0-2; Cowen's Baitfish, 2/0-4; Clouser Deep Minnow, 2/0-2; DuBiel's Lil'Hadden, 2/0-2; Lefty's Deceiver, 2/0-4; Parson's Tutti Fruiti, 2-4; Threadfin Shad, 1/0-2; Wirt's Redfish Rattler, 1/0-2.

When to Fish
September to mid-March for stripers. Spring and fall are the best times for all the rest. Summer can be ok if you do not mind boat traffic and jet skis.

Season and Limits
You can fish all year long. Practice catch and release. Mercury content has been found in some of these fish.

Nearby Fly Fishing
Lake Gaston, (connected to Kerr), or Falls Lake above Durham, North Carolina, are both close and can be quite productive.

Accommodations & Services
The city of Henderson is a short distance south of Kerr Lake. Bobcat's Bait and Tackle in Clarksville has gas without ethanol for boats. North Bend Park Pier has handicap access.

There are plenty of areas to gain access to the lake, including a few parks that provide camping and boat ramps. In North Carolina, boat access can be found at the Satterwhite Point Recreation Area, Hibernia, Henderson Point, County Line, and Nutbush Creek. Some favorite areas on the Virginia side include Occoneechee State Park, Ivy Hill Park, Grassy Creek, Island Creek Recreation Area, and Staunton River State Park.

Helpful Websites
www.bobcatslakecountry.com
www.virginia-outdoors.com

Rating
As a coldwater fishery, it is hard to beat the solitude. This is a vast reservoir that takes time to learn. I rate it an 8, but on a good day it can be a 10.

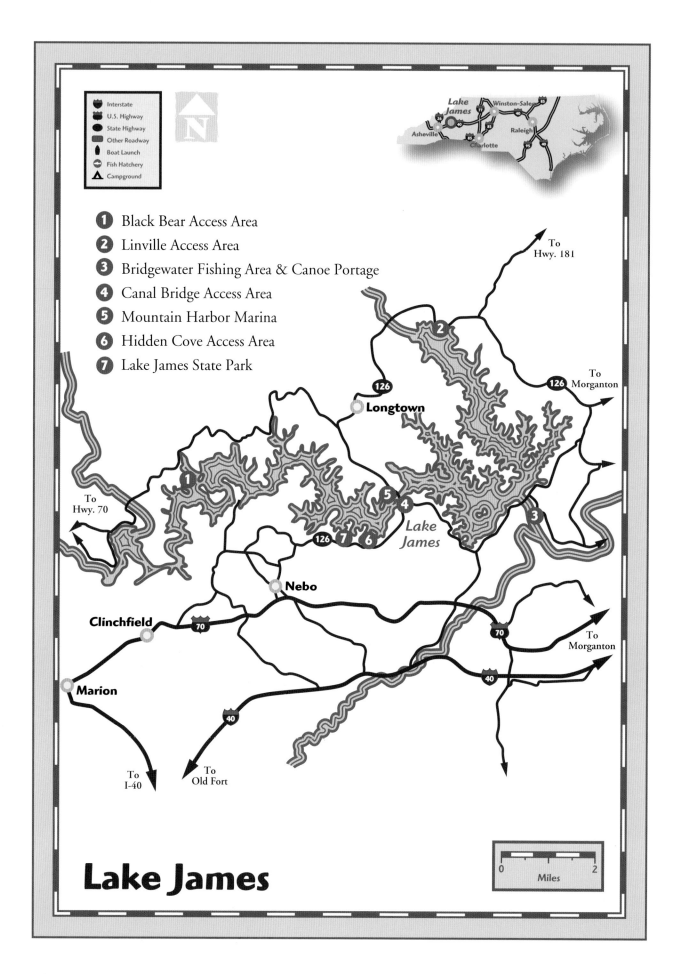

Legend:
- Interstate
- U.S. Highway
- State Highway
- Other Roadway
- Boat Launch
- Fish Hatchery
- Campground

1. Black Bear Access Area
2. Linville Access Area
3. Bridgewater Fishing Area & Canoe Portage
4. Canal Bridge Access Area
5. Mountain Harbor Marina
6. Hidden Cove Access Area
7. Lake James State Park

Lake James

Winston-Salem
Asheville
Raleigh
Charlotte

To Hwy. 181
To Morganton
Longtown
To Hwy. 70
Lake James
Nebo
Clinchfield
Marion
To Morganton
To I-40
To Old Fort

Miles
0   2

Lake James

Lake James

North Carolina boasts numerous lakes and reservoirs worthy of a fly fisher's attention. Buggs Island Lake and Falls Lake come to mind. However, the lake I chose for this volume has fishing to suit the taste of practically any angler. Lake James, about five miles northeast of Marion, is the most eastern of the big mountain lakes, and it features both warm and cold water and the diversity of fish that thrive in each environment. There are largemouth, smallmouth, hybrid, and white bass, and crappie and sunfish, as well as walleye and muskie.

The lake has two major sections. The Linville River flows through Linville Gorge and empties into this lake forming the colder northern arm. The Catawba River feeds the southern arm.

Lake James State Park, (Exit 90 on Interstate 40), features a rustic twenty-site, walk-in tent campground on the southern shore where I have been able to beach a canoe. There are also secluded islands to camp on, and enough wide-open space to create a sense of solitude.

White is the go-to color when fishing for smallmouth bass at Lake James.

Sunrise over the Blue Ridge Mountains at Lake James.

*An egret perches on a snag tree. The timber along the
banks of Lake James provides good cover for bass.*

Lake James was engineered as a hydroelectric reservoir named after Duke Energy founder, James B. Duke. As with most fishing destinations, it does take time to learn the rhythm of the place. An example of this was learning from a park ranger about going deep for the smallmouth bass that school up in the channel above the dam near the campground. One of the best times to catch them is at daybreak in the early spring. I used a 7-foot sinking-tip line with a short monofilament leader. White seems to be the go-to color for smallies, in the form of a weighted streamer such as a Woolly Bugger or Lefty's Deceiver. May is the spawning season for white bass. Likely places for bass in the lake include boat docks and bridge pilings. The fish are often found deep, at depths of thirty feet or more. The average depth of the lake is about forty-six feet depending on water levels, with some holes three times as deep.

Walleye, comfortable in deep cold water, were introduced in 1951. These fish can be found along the shallow bank edges during spring spawning season. The average size is ten to twelve inches; keepers must measure a minimum of 15 inches. Largemouth bass are usually found near the stumps, drop-offs, and other structures. The lake record for largemouth is more than fourteen pounds while the lake record for smallmouth is more than seven. Lake James also boasts state records for white catfish, northern pike, and tiger muskellunge. There are plenty of places to cast. The reservoir is quite expansive, encompassed by 150 miles of shoreline covering 6,500 acres, and the scenery is incredible.

While Lake James is popular with anglers and recreational users, it has even caught the imagination of Hollywood. Two major films have had numerous scenes filmed here including *The Last of the Mohicans* and *The Hunt for Red October*. During the making of *The Last of the Mohicans,* a huge set was constructed that depicted historic Fort William Henry on Lake George in the British Province of New York.

There is good access with several boat ramps on the lake. Black Bear Access is just off of Lake James Road on the western edge. The Linville Access area is on the top of the northern arm, off N.C. Highway 126 near the Linville River confluence. Canal Bridge on Highway 126 near the McDowell–Burke County line is right at the junction of the two arms.

The Bridgewater fishing area and canoe-portage tailrace on the Catawba River at the southeastern edge of Lake James is another area of interest to fly fishers. This section is operated in conjunction with the North Carolina Wildlife Resources Commission.

The upper mile of the Catawba River nearest the dam has a hatchery-supported population of trout. Farther downstream special regulations apply.

Types of Fish

Smallmouth bass, largemouth bass, carp, crappie, tiger muskie, walleye, striped bass, hybrid striped bass, bluegill, white bass, and white catfish.

Known Baitfish

Threadfin shad, gizzard shad, bluegill, redbreast, redear sunfish.

Equipment to Use

Rods: 5- to 9-weight, 8 to 9 feet in length.
Reels: Mechanical and palm.
Lines: Weight-forward floating matched to rod. Sinking-tip lines are also effective here.
Leaders: 3x to 5x leaders 9 feet in length or 3 or 4 feet for sinking-tip lines.
Wading: Wading is possible in some places on the shore but a boat, canoe, or kayak is best.

Flies to Use

Surface: Chernobyl Ant, sizes 8-10; Walt's Popper, 2-12; Wilkins's Fire Tiger, 4-8.

Subsurface: Chuck's Claw-Dad, sizes 2-6; Clouser Minnow, 1/0-6; Lefty's Half & Half, 1/0-6; Shenk's White Minnow, 4-6; Woolly Bugger, 4-8.

When to Fish

Late February through April is best for smallmouth bass. Largemouth and white bass can be caught in both spring and fall.

Season & Limits

Check with local game laws for creel limits.

Nearby Fly Fishing

The Linville River flows into the northeastern portion of the lake.

Accommodations & Services

The towns of Marion and Morganton are just a few miles away. Lake James State Park has walk-in tent sites.

Mountain Harbour Marina (828) 584-0666.

North Carolina Park Access (877) 722-6762.

Rating

Lake James is beautiful but fly fishing it can be a challenge. This is a great place to test yourself. I rate it a 7.

Lake James smallmouth bass have shoulders, and they utilize the great depths of the lake to make long diagonal and vertical runs.

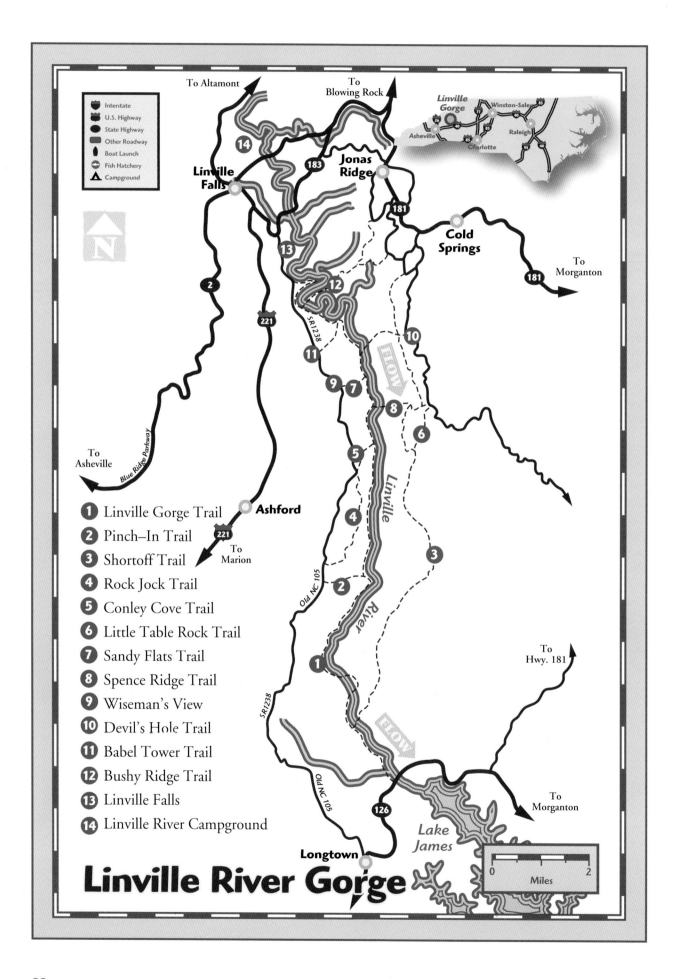

Legend

- Interstate
- U.S. Highway
- State Highway
- Other Roadway
- Boat Launch
- Fish Hatchery
- Campground

To Altamont

To Blowing Rock

Linville Gorge

Winston-Salem

Asheville

Charlotte

Raleigh

N

Linville Falls

183

Jonas Ridge

181

Cold Springs

181

To Morganton

2

221

13

12

SR1238

11

10

9 7

8

6

To Asheville

Blue Ridge Parkway

5

4

Linville River

Ashford

221

To Marion

Old NC 105

2

3

To Hwy. 181

1

1 Linville Gorge Trail
2 Pinch–In Trail
3 Shortoff Trail
4 Rock Jock Trail
5 Conley Cove Trail
6 Little Table Rock Trail
7 Sandy Flats Trail
8 Spence Ridge Trail
9 Wiseman's View
10 Devil's Hole Trail
11 Babel Tower Trail
12 Bushy Ridge Trail
13 Linville Falls
14 Linville River Campground

SR1238

Old NC 105

126

To Morganton

Lake James

Longtown

0 Miles 2

Linville River Gorge

Linville River Gorge

Linville Gorge. Just the name conjures up images of a mystical and epic place, but its early history was rooted in violence. An explorer, William Linville, and his son were scalped in 1776 near the river that bears his name. And if you've never been to Linville Gorge, there's a chance you've seen its dramatic cliffs and the river itself in *The Last of the Mohicans*. With headwaters high on Grandfather Mountain, the Linville works its way down over some magnificent falls. This place is so rugged that U.S. Army Rangers and other special forces have used it for mountaineering exercises.

After many months of planning, waiting, and looking forward to a backpacking-and-angling trip into the largest gorge east of the Mississippi, I finally found myself in the middle of it. I was not disappointed. Brandon Ball and his friends had been taking backpacking trips down here for years. He was my guide and briefed me on what to expect.

I traveled as a minimalist with only the most basic backpacking gear including a four-piece 4-weight fly rod. We worked our way down the incredibly steep Pinch In Trail pausing to observe the sheer magnitude of what the Cherokee people called *Eeseeoh,* meaning river of many cliffs.

The Linville River itself is littered with massive boulders and bordered with ancient forests of oak, hemlock, and white pine. The Linville Gorge Trail follows the river course for twelve miles.

A typical Linville River smallmouth.

Casting for smallies deep in the gorge.

There are numerous access trails from both rims, all very steep. They are only marked at the top; most are not well maintained. It is a wilderness area, and solo trips are *not* recommended.

During my trip, the rhododendron was in bloom and the fishing was hot. There was plenty of cover for our quarry—smallmouth bass. Yes, this may come as a surprise to those who think of the Linville River as a trout stream. There are some trout in there, but it is somewhat hatchery supported. But according to one of the state's leading conservationists, Morganton resident Michael "Squeak" Smith, "the water down in the gorge is just marginal." Smith, an avid sportsman, former fighter pilot, and national Trout Unlimited advocate, says the low trout numbers are due to all of the development just above the gorge. The numerous golf courses and resort construction have taken their toll, and the water temperature has gone up a few degrees. The fishing this past June was good, but it was all about the smallmouth bass. The Linville River Gorge is prime habitat for those tigers with fins. There was plenty of good action in numerous plunge pools and runs up and down the river. Any minnowlike fly was effective as were large surface flies. But what really got those bass excited were crayfish patterns. Most of the fish were in the ten- to fourteen-inch range but even the smaller ones are quite feisty on a 4-weight.

Upon my return up the canyon I parted from the pack for a taste of solitude and true wilderness experience. At rest near some big rocks, I witnessed a rare and serendipitous scene: a pair of peregrines soaring and stunt flying through the sky. I consider myself somewhat of a birder yet I had never before witnessed the caliber of raptor acrobatics that I saw that morning. Such episodes are just another reason I enjoy the fly-fishing experience. Regardless of the catch, the trip can offer glimpses of the natural world that only a few other endeavors can equal.

If you are considering a trip into Linville Gorge, it is highly recommended that you visit the Linville Falls Recreation & Visitor Center, open April 15 through November 1 from 9 to 5. The center is located at Mile Post 316 of the Blue Ridge Parkway between U.S. 221 and N.C. 181. Here the National Park Service rangers can answer questions and provide maps of the various routes down into the gorge.

Linville Falls Recreational Area.

Types of Fish
Mostly smallmouth bass, rock bass, some big brown trout, and some rainbow trout.

Known Hatches
Baetis, Black Caddis, Crawfish, Black Stonefly, Blue Quill, Blue-Winged Olive, Cream Midge, Gray Caddis, Gray Fox, Green Drake, Hendrickson, Isonychia, Light Cahill, March Brown, midge, Quill Gordon, Giant Stonefly, terrestrials, Yellow Midge, Yellow Stonefly.

Equipment to Use
Rods: 4- to 6-weight, 8½ to 9 feet long.
Reels: Standard mechanical.
Lines: Weight-forward floating, matched to rod.
Leaders: 4x to 5x leaders, 9 feet long.
Wading: If wet wading use good boots, chest waders if you do not mind hauling them down in your pack.

Flies To Use
Drys: Adams, sizes 16-22; Black Beetle, 14-16; Blue-Winged Olive Parachute, 14-20; Blue Quill, 14-18; Cahill, 14-20; Coffin Fly, 14-18; Dave's Hopper, 12-14; Elk-Hair Caddis, 16-18; Flying Ant, 12-18; Glo Bug, 14-18; Griffith's Gnat, 20; Hendrickson, 14-18; Humpy, 16-18; Inchworm, 14-18; Irresistible, 14-18; Little Yellow Sally, 14-20; March Brown, 16-18; Mosquito, 14-18; Olive Midge, 18-24; Quill Gordon, 12-20; Royal Coachman, 14-18; Royal Wulff, 14-18; Stimulator, 12-18.

Nymphs & Streamers: Brassie, sizes 14-18; Beadhead Pheasant Tail, 16-18; Beadhead Gold Ribbed Hare's Ear, 14-16; Beadhead Prince Nymphs, 14-18; Black Stonefly Nymph, 18; Big Nasty Crayfish, 4-8; Clouser Minnow, 6-8; Copper John, 14-18; Damsel, 14-16; Flashback Hare's Ear, 14-18; Gray Midge, 18-24; Little Prince Nymph, 16-18; March Brown Nymph, 16-18; MC2 Crayfish, size 4; Mickey Finn, 8-10; Muddler Minnow, 6-10; Pat's Nymph, 18-24; San Juan Worm, 14-16; Scud, 12-18; Sculpin, 6-8; Stone Nymph, 6-10; Woolly Bugger, 6-10; Y2K, 10.

When to Fish
May through October is ideal.

Season & Limits
The lower Linville River in the gorge is hatchery supported, see current restrictions. Most fly fishers catch and release the bass.

Nearby Fly Fishing
Wilson Creek is not too far away, and the Linville River is quite nice above the 85-foot falls.

Accommodations & Services
The towns of Marion and Morganton are your best bet for supplies. Linville Falls Campground near MP 316 (follow the signs) is a pleasant place to camp just off the Blue Ridge Parkway.

Rating
Wilderness fly fishing is always an adventure and this one rates a 9 in my book.

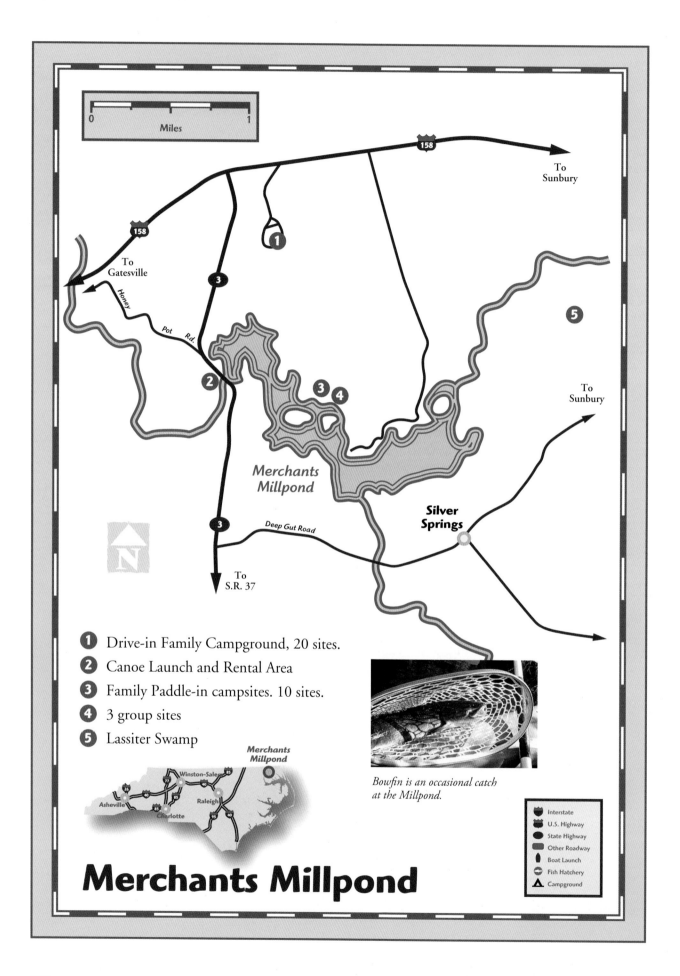

Miles
0 ... 1

158
To
Sunbury

158
To
Gatesville

Honey

Pot Rd.

1

3

2

3

4

5

Merchants
Millpond

Silver
Springs

To
Sunbury

Deep Gut Road

N

To
S.R. 37

① Drive-in Family Campground, 20 sites.

② Canoe Launch and Rental Area

③ Family Paddle-in campsites. 10 sites.

④ 3 group sites

⑤ Lassiter Swamp

Merchants
Millpond

Winston-Salem
Asheville
Charlotte
Raleigh

Bowfin is an occasional catch
at the Millpond.

Symbol	Type
	Interstate
	U.S. Highway
	State Highway
	Other Roadway
	Boat Launch
	Fish Hatchery
△	Campground

Merchants Millpond

Merchants Millpond State Park

"They've got bass in there as big as your leg," a local fellow told me years ago when I was inquiring about the fishing possibilities at Merchants Millpond State Park, which is in the extreme northeastern part of the state. It is a black-water ecosystem consisting of coastal pond and southern swamp forest dominated by Spanish moss-covered bald cypress and water tupelo trees. The millpond is a wondrous place for practitioners of the "quiet sport." It is not uncommon to witness a beaver gliding through the lily pads, watch a prothonotary warbler with a beak full of bugs, or observe the splash of a largemouth as it explodes on a hovering dragonfly.

Gates County was settled in 1660. As time went on the millpond became the center of trade. Lumber, gristmills, farm supplies, and a sawmill contributed to the evolution of the name: Merchants Millpond. In 1973, with help from generous contributors, including the Nature Conservancy, Merchants Millpond became a state park that now covers more than 3,000 acres.

The author probes the pond near the canoe campsite. Photo by Elizabeth Larson.

The business end of a chain pickerel.

Canoes and kayaks are the best way to navigate the waters of Merchants Millpond.

This swampy and mysterious place is home to a unique and diverse population of birds, fish, and other aquatic creatures. There are 37 known species of fish including such prehistoric species as bowfins, chain pickerel, and alligator gar. The most predominant predators are largemouth bass and black crappie. The Millpond fish population has rebounded well after being ravaged by Hurricane Isabelle in 2003.

The spring is my favorite time to visit, when one can watch the warblers build their nests between casts. Summer can be a bit buggy and the vegetation gets thick. In late April or May, paddle out. target a submerged log, and cast your fly right beside it. Avoid overhanging limbs on your backcast. This place is all about flat-water surface action.

Crawfish or floating frog-like poppers work well, as do dragonfly or damselfly imitations. Terrestrials such as ants, beetles, or cicadas are a good bet. Streamers that look like salamanders open up all sorts of possibilities. Almost any big fly or popping bug that floats deserves consideration here. Be sure to use a stout rod, floating line, and big bass-size hook with a monofilament grass guard if possible. There is plenty of duckweed, mosquito fern, and parrot feather that can foul up your fly line.

Kayaks, canoes, or johnboats are the best way to get around here. Electric trolling motors are allowed but not necessary. There are a few 15- to 16-foot holes but with an average depth of 3- to 5-feet, underwater cypress knees and submerged stumps could wreak havoc on your propeller. The state park rents canoes on an hourly or daily basis. There are three camping areas. One section is set back from the pond and offers drive-up campsites. There are two overnight paddle-camp sections that have more of a wilderness feel. A series of family sites and a series of group campsites are situated just off the water. One could easily get lost were it not for the well-marked buoy trails. There is also a remote paddle trail that winds from the Millpond deep into 1,000-acre Lassiter Swamp. Oh, by the way, beware—this is gator country. At last count there were at least three alligators thriving in the park.

The author examines a Millpond bass. Photo by Elizabeth Larson.

Prothonotary warblers are commonly observed here in the spring. They feed on the prolific insect life and line their nests with Spanish moss.

Types of Fish
Largemouth bass, chain pickerel, bluegill, bowfin, long-nosed gar, and black crappie.

Known Hatches
The best forage includes dragonflies, damselflies, frogs, tadpoles, salamanders, and crickets.

Equipment to Use
Rods: 4- to 8-weight, 8 to 9 feet in length.
Reels: Standard mechanical.
Line: Weight-forward, floating matched to rod.
Leaders: 2x through 5x, 9 feet in length.
Wading: Kayaks, canoes, and other small boats work best here, trolling motors are susceptible to submerged logs.

Flies to Use
Topwater flies are my first preference here due to the density of aquatic vegetation.

Surface: Braided Butt Damsel, sizes 8-12; DP Popper, 2-6; DP Slider, 4-6; Dave's Hopper, 2-6; Foam Damsel, 6-12; Walt's Frog Slider, 2-6; Whitlock's Deer Hair Popper, 4-6; Wilkins's Ultra Foam Fire Tiger Bass Popper, 4-6.

Subsurface: Carter's Rubber-Legged Dragon, sizes 2-6; Chocklett's Gummy Minnow, 2-6; Chuck's Claw-Dad, Brown, 4-6; Clouser Crayfish, 2-6; Conehead Bugger, 4-8; Clouser Deep Minnow, 4-6; Muddler Minnow, 2-8; Woolly Bugger, 2-12.

When to Fish
The best fishing is from April to October.

Season & Limits
Year-round. Note gas motors are not allowed.

Nearby Fly Fishing
The Chowan River is about 30 minutes west on Highway 158.

The Weldon boat launch on the Roanoke River is about an hour west.

Accommodations & Services
Camping within the state park, both drive-up and canoe campsites.

Rating
Even if the fishing is slow, you cannot go wrong here. Merchants Millpond rates an 8.

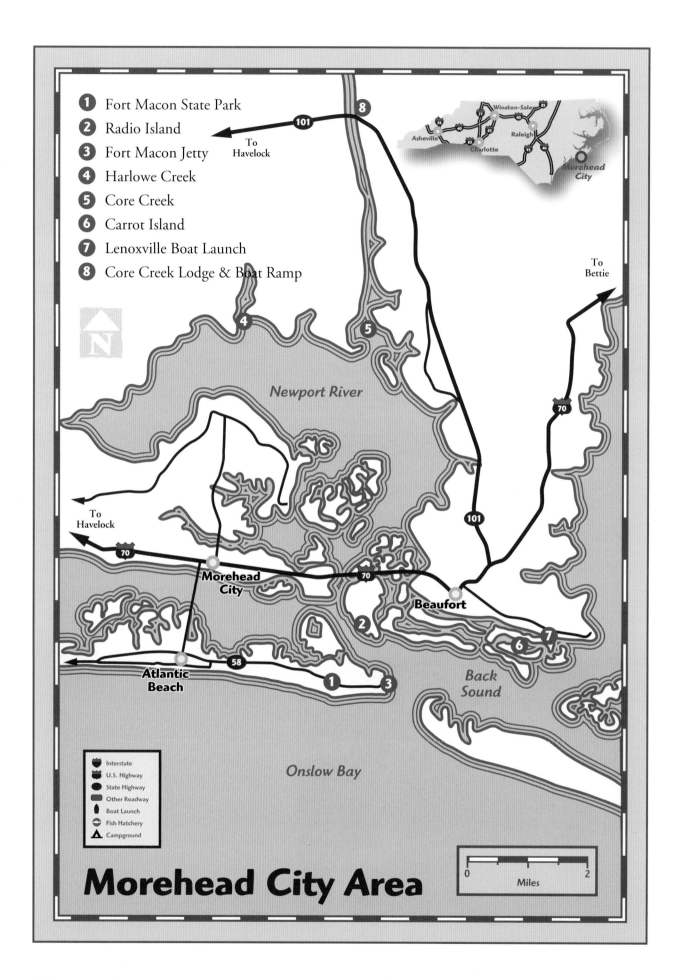

1 Fort Macon State Park
2 Radio Island
3 Fort Macon Jetty
4 Harlowe Creek
5 Core Creek
6 Carrot Island
7 Lenoxville Boat Launch
8 Core Creek Lodge & Boat Ramp

To Havelock

To Bettie

Newport River

Morehead City

Beaufort

Atlantic Beach

Back Sound

Onslow Bay

Interstate
U.S. Highway
State Highway
Other Roadway
Boat Launch
Fish Hatchery
Campground

0 Miles 2

Morehead City Area

Morehead City Area

apt. Gordon Churchill guided the flats boat along with a push pole, while keeping a keen eye out for the telltale wake or V-shaped push of North Carolina's state fish: the red drum. This kind of fly fishing is akin to hunting. Chasing reds on these backwater creeks requires patience, stealth, and steady nerves. Churchill knows the difference between the sounds of mullet splashing and a redfish busting bait. He explained that precise casting is a must and that presentations must look authentic—close enough to catch the fish's eye but not so close as to spook it. In terms of placement, below and to one side of the feeding red's snout is ideal. We moved through water that was as shallow as six inches in places.

The tidal creeks and salt marshes are ideal to explore by kayak or other shallow-draft boats.

Tails, You Win

Although we were sight fishing, the marshy backwaters where Churchill maneuvers his shallow-draft boat are often murky.

Fly fishing for redfish, even a puppy drum such as this one, requires skill, stealth, and patience. Photo by David Dow.

Morehead City is surrounded by shallow backwaters. Many are ideal for stalking redfish with a shallow-draft boat. If you were to try to wade here, you might sink to your ears.

Similar to stalking tailing bonefish, the excitement of fishing on these redfish flats ratchets up a few notches when you can actually see the tails of the fish as they scour the muddy bottom, nose down, for crabs, shrimp, mullet, and other morsels of food. Many of the reds in this area are not puppy drum, but brutish fish with shoulders, easily exceeding the size of most bonefish.

There are hundreds of places around Morehead City, including Bogue Sound and the Newport River, to stalk redfish or spottails, the local name for these much sought-after fish. Most of the water here is over soft bottom, so wading is not advised, but the vast acreage of marsh grass creates an ideal tidal estuary that can be fished in shallow-draft boats if you're knowledgeable about the tides. There is a good boat ramp in Beaufort, the state's third-oldest city, at the end of Taylors Creek, just off U.S. 70 on Lennoxville Road. The Morehead City ramp is on the main drag behind the visitor center, about 2.7 miles east of the U.S. 70 and N.C. 24 intersection.

Of course red drum are not the only prize. Speckled trout, locally referred to as specks, are another popular target in the drum family. They are abundant, especially in the fall. Flounder, Spanish mackerel, and croaker are in the mix during the warmer months. Some favorite haunts worth checking out include but are not limited to the Haystacks (aka Newport Marshes just northwest of the bridge between Morehead City and Beaufort), Beaufort Inlet, the Radio Island Jetty, Harlow Creek, Core Creek, the Fort Macon area including Fort Macon Jetty, and Carrot Island, which is a part of the Rachel Carson Nature Preserve.

Capt. Matt Wirt's Redfish Rattler fly.

Terns, gulls, and other seabirds can be a good indicator of where the action is.

Types of Fish
Red drum, black drum, false albacore, bluefish, speckled trout, croaker, and flounder.

Known Baitfish
Anglers on the Lower Cape Fear can expect finger mullet, menhaden, shrimp, crabs, and other small baitfish.

Flies to Use
Bend Back, sizes 1/0-2; Bruce's Crystal Shrimp, 1/0; Chocklett's Gummy Minnow, 2/0-2; Clouser Minnow, 2/0-2; Cowen's Baitfish, 1/0; DuBiel's Finesse Fly, 2-4; DuBiel's Lil' Hadden, 1/0-2; DuBiel's Red-Ducer, 1/0-2; Lefty's Deceiver, 2/0-2; Lefty's Half & Half, 3/0-1/0; Popovics's Surf Candy, 1/0; Tommy's Crease Fly, 1/0-2; Tommy's Eel Fly, 2/0-1/0; Trow's Minnow, 3/0-6; Walt's Saltwater Popper, 1/0-2; Wirt's Redfish Rattler, 2/0-2; Wirt's Shark Fly, 3/0.

When to Fish
Spring, fall, and summer are the most productive times.

Season & Limits
Open all year long. Consult the North Carolina Wildlife Resources Commission website (listed below) for regulations and slot limits.

Nearby Fly Fishing
Cape Lookout, Bogue Sound, Bear Island, Cedar Island area, Shackleford Banks, and Harkers Island.

Accommodations & Services
There is a plethora of accommodations and services in both Morehead City and nearby Beaufort. There are also many competent guides who know the waterways that could be treacherous to a novice.

Helpful Web Sites
www.ncwildlife.org
www.nccoastchamber.com
www.capelookoutflyshop.com

Rating
There is a lifetime of great fly-fishing potential in this diverse area and I rate it a 9.

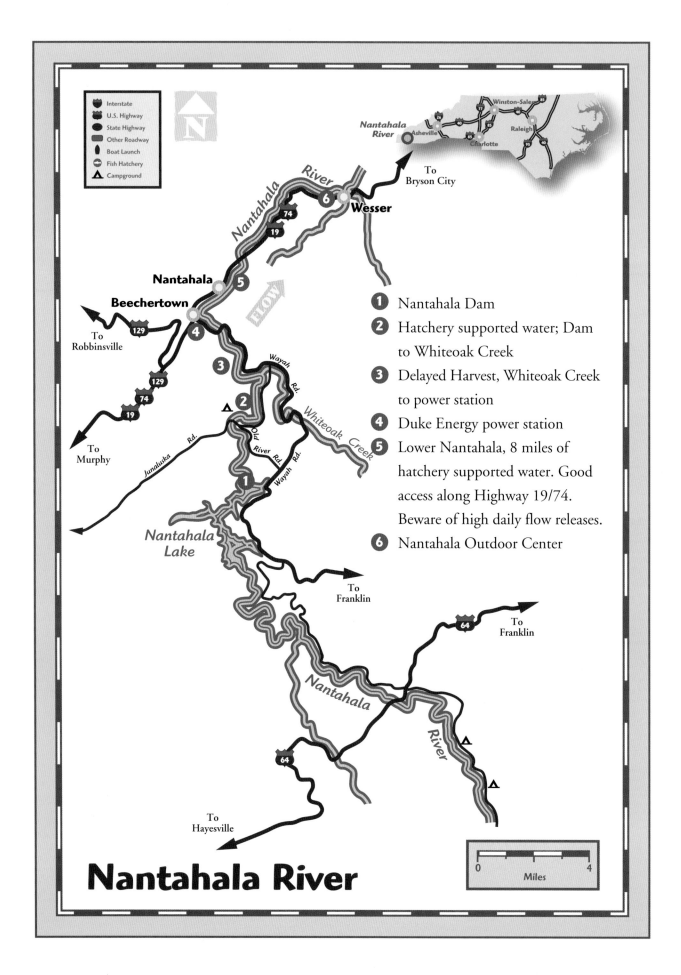

Legend:
- Interstate
- U.S. Highway
- State Highway
- Other Roadway
- Boat Launch
- Fish Hatchery
- Campground

N

Nantahala River

To Bryson City

Winston-Salem

Asheville

Raleigh

Charlotte

Wesser

74

19

6

Nantahala

5

Beechertown

129

To Robbinsville

4

74

19

To Murphy

3

Wayah Rd.

Junaluska Rd.

2

Old River Rd.

Wayah Rd.

Whiteoak Creek

1

Nantahala Lake

To Franklin

64

To Franklin

Nantahala River

64

To Hayesville

1 Nantahala Dam

2 Hatchery supported water; Dam to Whiteoak Creek

3 Delayed Harvest, Whiteoak Creek to power station

4 Duke Energy power station

5 Lower Nantahala, 8 miles of hatchery supported water. Good access along Highway 19/74. Beware of high daily flow releases.

6 Nantahala Outdoor Center

0   Miles   4

Nantahala River

Nantahala River

My first visit to Nantahala River Gorge as an adult rekindled some childhood memories. There was something familiar about first hearing and then seeing the Great Smoky Mountains Scenic Railroad wind its way through the trees above the river like a giant colorful snake.

The Cherokee people appreciated the beauty and bounty of this place and named it *Nantahala,* meaning land of the noonday sun. Shadowed by towering gorge walls, the river has long been considered one of North Carolina's most popular outdoor playgrounds and one of finest rivers in the Southeast. From Bryson City, U.S. Highway 19/74 provides access to the gorge and follows the southern side of the river through Macon and Swain counties.

Camping along the high banks of the Nantahala with some members of the Nat Greene Flyfishers Club out of Greensboro proved to be a wise decision. The years of experience among the members represented a vast pool of knowledge. We fished together, shared a campfire, and I observed some highly skilled anglers who helped contribute valuable information to this book.

A fine trout typical of those found in the Nantahala.

Watch out for trains in the lower gorge section of the Nantahala.

Fish on! A battle in the fast water for angler Clarence "Rock" Rothrock.

There are three sections to fish here. The most popular is the delayed-harvest section, a four-mile stretch on Wayah Road above the power generating plant. Heading upstream, turn left off U.S. 19 at the Nantahala River Launch Site Recreation Area. The stream here is narrow, and much of it can be fished from the banks. This section has high fish counts and good turnout access. The splashy lower section is the last eight miles of the gorge. This hatchery-supported tailwater attracts hordes of rafters, kayakers, and canoers during the warm months. Water is periodically released through a huge pipe from Nantahala Lake. Because of all the "splash and gigglers" traffic by day, this is one of the few places you can legally fish at night, and the legal area is from the Swain County line downstream. The best time to fish the lower river is when the water is down and before the boats arrive. There are a few important caveats. Take caution while wading on the lower section as water levels can rise without notice. Also be aware of the train schedule. You might find yourself hiking near the railroad tracks at precisely the same time as the train approaches. Be aware that the canyon walls and gurgling rapids can mask the sound of the train.

Do not underestimate the fishing potential of this river, which produced the state-record brown trout, landed by Robert Dyer in the spring of 1998. The leviathan weighed in at 24 pounds 10 ounces.

Farther up the road above the delayed-harvest section, the rhododendron-and-mountain-laurel-lined headwaters offer wild brook trout for the purist. Observe the posted signs for special regulations on the tributaries.

The caddis hatch is particularly strong on the Nantahala during the late spring into mid-July. There is also a special traditional fly associated with the Nantahala River, known as the Yellow Hammer, or as the locals call it, *Yallerhammer*. This striking fly was originally tied with feathers from a yellow-shafted flicker and imitates those pesky yellow jackets. I am anxious to get back on the "Nanny," and that is precisely the fly I would like to try.

Lorraine Rothrock, on a trip with Nat Greene Flyfishers.

Types of Fish

The Nantahala is one of the most versatile streams in the state offering plenty of feisty brook trout, some wild rainbows, and some nice browns.

Known Hatches

Baetis, Black Caddis, Crawfish, Black Stonefly, Blue Quill, Blue-Winged Olive, Cream Midge, Gray Caddis, Gray Fox, Green Drake, Hendrickson, Isonychia, Light Cahill, March Brown, midge, Quill Gordon, Giant Stonefly, Sulfur, terrestrials, Yellow Midge, Yellow Stonefly.

Equipment to Use

Rods: 3- to 5-weight, 8 to 9 feet in length.
Reels: Standard
Lines: Weight-forward floating.
Wading: Chest waders are recommended, however hip waders, bank fishing, and wet-wading with good wading footwear is fine.

Flies:

Drys: Adams, sizes 16-18; Black Beetle, 14-16; Blue Thorax Dun, 18-22; Blue-Winged Olive Parachute, 16-20; Blue Quill, 14-18; Cahill, 14-20; Coffin Fly, 14-18; Dave's Hopper, 12-14; Elk-Hair Caddis, 14-18; Flying Ant, 12-18; Glo Bug, 14-18; Griffith's Gnat, 20; Gray Midge, 18-22; Hendrickson, 14-18; Humpy, 16-18; Inchworm, 14-18; Irresistible, 14-18; Little Yellow Sally, 14-20; March Brown, 16-18; Mosquito, 14-18; Quill Gordon, 12-20; Royal Coachman, 14-18; Royal Wulff, 14-18; Stimulator, 12-18; Thunderhead, 12-16; Yellow Hammer, 10-14.

Nymphs & Streamers: Brassie, sizes 14-18; Beadhead Pheasant Tail, 16-18; Beadhead Gold Ribbed Hare's Ear, 14-16; Bullethead Grasshopper, size 10; Copper John, 14-18; Damsel, 14-16; Flashback Hare's Ear, 14-18; Gray Ghost, 8-12; Little Prince Nymph, 16-18; March Brown Nymph, 16-18; Mickey Finn, 8-10; Muddler Minnow, 6-10; Pat's Nymph, 18-24; San Juan Worm, 14-16; Scud, 12-18; Sculpin, 6-8; Stone Nymph, 6-10; Woolly Bugger, 6-10.

When to Fish

The best time to fish is early spring and fall.

Season & Limits

Consult current regulations for different sections of the river and its tributaries, which include hatchery supported, delayed harvest, and wild trout sections. Catch and release is recommended.

Nearby Flyfishing

Deep Creek is another fine stream in the Smokies just outside of Bryson City.

Accommodations & Services

Nantahala Outdoor Center is convenient for basic supplies located right there on the river, on U.S. 19 about thirteen miles west of Bryson City. Bryson City has a nice variety of amenities. Brookside Creek Campground in Topton (1-800-848-7238) is one of many convenient places to camp near the river.

Rating

I rate the Nantahala an 8, as the trout are plentiful and this scenic river has lots of good access points.

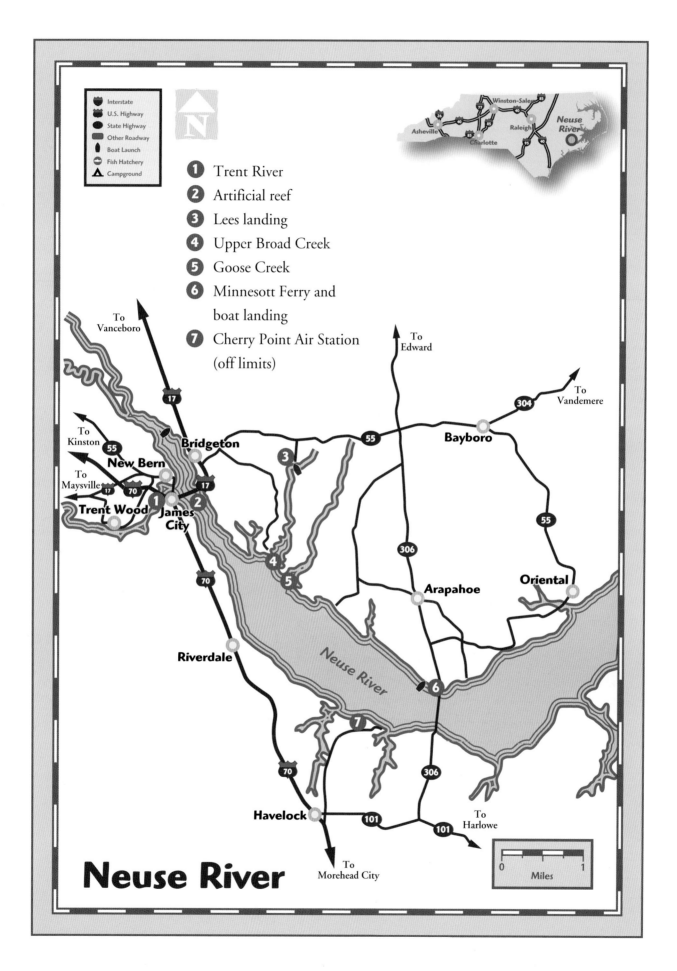

Legend:
- Interstate
- U.S. Highway
- State Highway
- Other Roadway
- Boat Launch
- Fish Hatchery
- Campground

1 Trent River
2 Artificial reef
3 Lees landing
4 Upper Broad Creek
5 Goose Creek
6 Minnesott Ferry and boat landing
7 Cherry Point Air Station (off limits)

Neuse River

To Vanceboro
To Edward
To Vandemere
To Kinston
To Maysville
Bridgeton
Bayboro
New Bern
Trent Wood
James City
Oriental
Arapahoe
Riverdale
Neuse River
Havelock
To Harlowe
To Morehead City
Miles

Neuse River

Neuse River

How many times in my youth did I cross that long-spanning bridge in New Bern, North Carolina, on my way from Greenville to Morehead City or Atlantic Beach. I crossed it going and coming without realizing what a treasure trove of angling potential abided in the waters just below. Fortunately, I found the right guide to help unlock some of the spectacular secrets of the Neuse.

His name is Capt. Gary Dubiel. Even if you are only a casual fly fisher, there is a good chance you may have heard of him or even seen him on ESPN or on the *Carolina Outdoor Journal*. He is famous for his knowledge of the region's waters, his saltwater fly creations, and prowess with a fly rod.

The Neuse River has the widest mouth of any river—five miles wide—in the continental United States. It is also gateway to the southern end of the Pamlico Sound. There is so much water in this region that it is hard to know where to begin. We started in one of the many large creeks that empty into the Neuse.

On an overcast drizzly morning, we wound our way to a woody area at the mouth of Broad Creek. Among the wide variety of

A selection of Capt. Gary Dubiel's hand-tied saltwater flies.

Jill, a regular client of Captain Dubiel's, took this redfish on a fly after sight-casting to it near the village of Oriental, which is also known as the Gateway to the Pamlico Sound.

Captain Dubiel hooked this three-year-old striper on the Neuse near New Bern.

birds, including ducks and gulls, we saw a blue heron perched on one of many old weathered stumps that provide cover for the baitfish and ambush points for red drum, striped bass, speckled sea trout, flounder, and even white perch.

One of the many interesting things about the Neuse River is the fact that it is a coastal river influenced more by wind than by tide. Also the salt content of the water fluctuates, thereby producing a fishery that can be unpredictable unless you have the knowledge of a local expert. And that morning, we dealt with a northeasterly wind, but beyond a point on the leeward side, we fished in relatively calm shallow water. Captain Gary elected to try some popping bugs on the surface.

Later that morning we worked our way up the Neuse to within a couple miles of the iconic bridges of New Bern. There, in the middle of the river, Captain Dubiel told me about an artificial reef below us, made from old truck tires and the like. The depth down to the reef ranged from about 10 to 14 feet, covering an expansive surface area of several hundred yards. The large yellow buoys that marked the area of the reef were arrayed in the shape of a big triangle. There was only one other boat fishing the area. The wind had let up, and we drifted over the reef, pushed by the current. Periodically we sight-cast to bursts of baitfish on the surface. It did not take long to learn that a school of striped bass was causing all the panic as it attacked the baitfish, which scattered across the top when they ran out of water. We had quite a few hook-ups, and many of the stripers were three-year-old fish, including one that had been tagged.

Soon enough, the boat we had seen earlier disappeared and we had the reef to ourselves. I could have stayed there all day, but Captain Dubiel had some other potential hotspots in close proximity to New Bern, including the nearby smaller and deeper Trent River. Overall it was an eye-opening tour that showed me what a rich and prolific fishery this is.

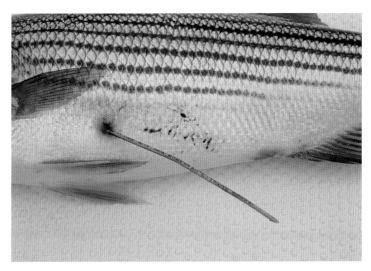

This tagged striper's information was recorded, and the fish was promptly released. The tag number was later reported to North Carolina marine wildlife authorities. Tagging programs provide invaluable data on the well-being of our state's fisheries.

Capt. Gary Dubiel casts for stripers—but it could just as easily be redfish or sea trout—near the mouth of Broad Creek on the Neuse.

Types of Fish

Fly fishers can target stripers, speckled trout, Spanish mackerel, flounder, red drum, hickory shad, white perch, largemouth bass, and the occasional bluefish mixed in.

Known Baitfish

Mullet, menhaden, shrimp, and smaller fishes.

Equipment to Use

Rods: 5- to 8-weight, 8 to 9 feet in length.
Reels: A large-arbor saltwater reel with a disc drag.
Lines: Floating, weight-forward to match rod weight, also intermediate and sinking-tip lines.
Leaders: 7- to 9-foot floating lines. 3- to 5-foot leaders of 20-pound test for sinking lines.
Wading: Bay boats are best, but canoes and kayaks can work well also.

Flies to Use

Bend Back, sizes 1/0-2; Bruce's Crystal Shrimp, 1/0; Clouser Minnow, 2/0-4; DuBiel's Finesse Fly, 2-4; DuBiel's Lil'Hadden, 1/0-2; DuBiel's Grey Fox, 1/0-2; Lefty's Deceiver, 2/0-2; Lefty's Half & Half, 2/0-2; Popovics's Surf Candy, 1/0; Tommy's Crease Fly, 2/0-2; Tommy's Eel Fly, 2/0-1/0; Trow's Saltwater Minnow, 3/0-6; Wilkins's Ultra Foam Fire Tiger Bass Popper, 1/0-2; Wirt's Redfish Rattler. 2/0-2.

When to Fish

All months except February are productive here.

Season and Limits

Various regulations and slot sizes are dependent on species. For current rules visit: www.ncwildlife.org.

Nearby Fly Fishing

Dawson, Goose, Hancock, and Broad Creeks, Trent River, and the Pamlico Sound.

Accommodations & Services

New Bern and the town of Oriental offer a plentiful array of stores, supplies, motels, and bed & breakfasts.

Helpful Website

www.specfever.com

Rating

With an incredible variety of water and species, this area is a solid 9.

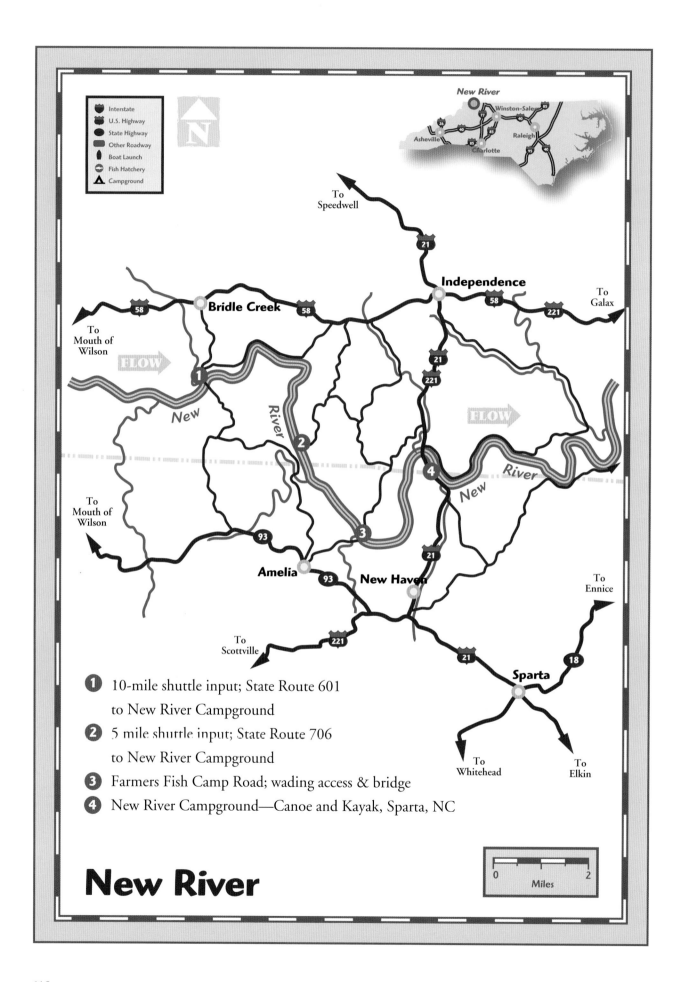

Legend:
- Interstate
- U.S. Highway
- State Highway
- Other Roadway
- Boat Launch
- Fish Hatchery
- Campground

N

New River

Winston-Salem
Asheville
Charlotte
Raleigh

To Speedwell

21

Independence

58   Bridle Creek   58

58   To Galax
221

To Mouth of Wilson

FLOW

21
221

1

New   River

FLOW

4   New   River

93

To Mouth of Wilson

3

Amelia   93   New Haven

21

To Scottville   221

221

21   Sparta   18

To Whitehead   To Elkin

To Ennice

1 10-mile shuttle input; State Route 601 to New River Campground

2 5 mile shuttle input; State Route 706 to New River Campground

3 Farmers Fish Camp Road; wading access & bridge

4 New River Campground—Canoe and Kayak, Sparta, NC

New River

0   Miles   2

New River

The New River is actually quite ancient. This is a fly fisher's Valhalla, with a nod to my Viking heritage and the Norse gods. North-flowing, this broad and brawling serpentine river shares the border with Virginia. Here, it is easy to lose track of which state you are in, due to a frenzied state of smallie fever.

My favorite single-day drift begins and ends at the New River Campground, simply because they have a great shuttle arrangement. For a nominal fee, the fine folks there will transport your canoe or kayak to a put-in location either five- or ten-miles upstream. If you need to rent one, they will provide that too. Then you are on your own as you work your way downstream negotiating some relatively mild (up to Class III) white water. There are plenty of calm stretches, islands, and boulder-strewn runs. The scenery ranges from pastoral to grand. Wildlife, such as deer and turkey or pileated woodpeckers and kingfishers, are common. The water is home to muskie, redeye rock bass, a few brown trout, catfish, sunfish, and even carp. The most-popular quarry is, of course, the indomitable smallmouth bass, or as my friend, guide Jeff Wilkins, describes them, "Tigers with fins."

During the summer, when the coastal fishing and trout action slows down on the eastern and western ends of the state, respectively, it just might be a good time to head up toward Sparta,

A nice fly selection for smallmouth, courtesy of Theo Copeland of the Appalachian Angler fly shop.

Dragonflies are prolific along the New River, and a well-crafted imitation of one would make a tempting target for a smallmouth bass.

North Carolina, barely more than a couple of hours drive from Greensboro. The New River Campground is located on U.S. Highway 21, just south of Independence on the Virginia border.

My old flat-bottom 14-foot Mad River Duck Hunter canoe has proven to be ideal for this type of fishing. One year during a major drought, the water levels got so low that my bow and stern really got raked over the rocks. Fortunately, installing skid plates put a new lease on its life.

Here are a few caveats if you decide to paddle. Do not canoe during a drought. Fasten rope on both ends of your vessel—you may need to pull it through some shallows or secure it to a bank. I have been known to harness the rope around my body when I find a good spot to fish among some shallow shoals. Be sure to bring an extra paddle and secure it inside the boat with bungee cords. Carry sunscreen and a hat, polarized sunglasses, and dry bags for cameras and such. Thunderstorms can appear suddenly in the mountains. I consider this a rule rather than an exception and I always bring rain gear. Wet wading is a great way to stay cool in the summer, and you can get in on same great smallie action this way. I like to get out of the boat and fish the islands and other likely places.

Woolly Buggers, Muddler Minnows, Girdle Bugs, and patterns that imitate crawfish, leeches, hellgramites, and a nice assortment of poppers and sliders will attract the bronzebacks. You'll also want to have some terrestrial patterns in your fly box, such as grasshoppers, crickets, and cicadas. You can often get away with a stout 2x tippet using 6- to 8-weight floating lines. As largemouth bass prefer logs, smallmouths love the rocks and boulders. Early morning is ideal for topwater action on the New River. Deeper pools and slow runs are worth extra attention, they may be home to big browns or a mammoth muskie. This is one type of water where an intermediate sinking-tip line would work well.

One final note—enjoy the grandeur of this primeval place but please—no more jokes about banjo music.

A Canada goose guards its nest on one of New River's multitude of small islands.

Types of Fish

Smallmouth bass are the prime target with populations of redeye rock bass, muskie, sunfish, carp, and flathead catfish.

Known Hatches

Think big terrestrials such as ants, beetles, crickets, cicadas, inchworms, and grasshoppers. Smallies also love crawfish, dragonflies, damselflies, frogs, hellgrammites, leeches, tadpoles, minnows, and small sunfish, including redbreast and bluegills.

Equipment to Use

Rods: 6- to 8-weight, 9 to 9½ feet in length.
Reels: Standard mechanical.
Lines: Weight-forward floating, matched to rod, also sinking-tip lines for deeper pools and runs.
Leaders: 1x to 2x leaders, 7½ to 9 feet in length, and 3 to 4 feet in length for sinking-tip lines.
Wading: Canoe or kayakers can wet wade in summer or float with a guide.

Flies to Use

Surface: Beetle, sizes 6-10; Dave's Cricket, 4-8; Dave's Hopper, 4-8; Walt's Frog Slider, 4-8; Walt's Popper, 4-8; Wilkins's Fire Tiger, 4-8.

Subsurface: Big Nasty Crayfish, sizes 2-6; Clouser Crayfish, 2-6; Clouser Minnow, 1/0-6; Dahlberg Diver, 4-8; Lefty's Deceiver, 2-10; Lefty's Half & Half, 1/0-4; MC2 Crayfish, 4; Muddler Minnow, 4-8; San Juan Worm, 8-12; Sculpin, 4-8; Skilton's Hellgrammite, 4-8; Woolly Bugger, 6-8; Zonker, 6-8; Beadhead Zug Bug, 6-10.

When to Fish

From May to early October are the best times.

Season & Limits

Check the regulations. A North Carolina fishing license or Virginia license is valid in the aforementioned shuttle section of the New River or up to 21 miles from the border.

Nearby Fly Fishing

Helton Creek and Stone Mountain State Park in Ashe County are not too far away.

Accommodations & Services

New River Campground is where I like to stay when doing the shuttle trip. They have a store, tackle, cottage, and boat rentals. Sparta is the biggest town just ten miles south of New River Campground. Independence is a smaller town, just north a few miles up the road across the Old Dominion border.

Rating

This is a superb smallmouth fly-fishing destination that deserves a solid 9.

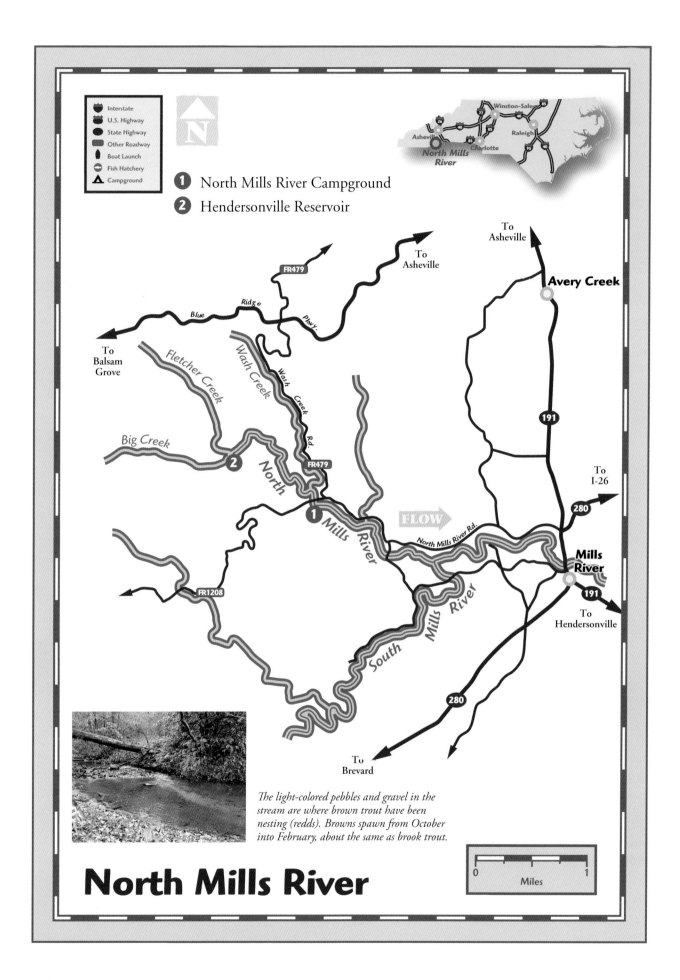

Legend

- Interstate
- U.S. Highway
- State Highway
- Other Roadway
- Boat Launch
- Fish Hatchery
- Campground

N

1 North Mills River Campground
2 Hendersonville Reservoir

To Asheville

Avery Creek

To Asheville

FR479

Blue Ridge Pkwy.

To Balsam Grove

Fletcher Creek

Wash Creek

Wash Creek Rd.

Big Creek

North

2

FR479

1

Mills River

FLOW

North Mills River Rd.

191

To I-26

280

Mills River

191

To Hendersonville

FR1208

South Mills River

280

To Brevard

The light-colored pebbles and gravel in the stream are where brown trout have been nesting (redds). Browns spawn from October into February, about the same as brook trout.

0   Miles   1

North Mills River

North Mills River

It was the week of Thanksgiving, and many families were busy traveling, shopping, or otherwise occupied with the holiday. I, however, was out exploring the North Mills River, a tributary to the French Broad River in Henderson County. This fine little delayed-harvest stream was running clear and low. The campground was closed but nearby a family harvested corn from a small patch tucked at the base of a mountain. It was one, two, three bears that I spotted while crossing a bridge. Omnivorous opportunists, the bears were taking full advantage of the holiday feast. Warily, I watched from a distance for a while and then took a walk along the streamside.

I met another fly fisher with a wary eye on the bears, a retired professor who explained that the North Mills was his home river, and he lived only 15 minutes away but that he had never before seen a bear in the wild. He was a member of the Trout Unlimited chapter in Asheville, an active group that acts as caretakers of the stream. As with other chapters of TU in the Tarheel State, they coordinate periodic stream cleanups and assist the North Carolina Wildlife Resources Commission with stocking activities.

Walker Parrott's fly box contains a winter collection of mini-midge patterns and assorted micro-flies that work well in ultra-clear mountain streams such as the Davidson and North Mills rivers.

Carey Kirk, patient professor, hooks a rainbow on a tiny midge pattern.

Near the forest campground, a view of the North Mills River, which runs low in November.

Pooling Our Resources

My new friend showed me a large pool that he says sees regular activity from poachers who harvest fish illegally. On this overcast day, however, we had the pool to ourselves. I watched him fish and told him, "I've got your back; I'll watch for bears."

The trout were feeding on tiny emergers. Splashy swirls just below surface marked them as targets. This kind of technical fishing, reminiscent of the nearby Davidson River, requires an extremely fine (7x) tippet, and in this case, the professor tied on a tiny size 22 midge. After numerous casts, he decided to switch to an even tinier size 24 fly. That was the ticket, and I watched as he caught and released a handsome rainbow trout.

Later I probed another stretch of the stream on my own, using a size 16 Blue-Winged Olive as a strike indicator above a size 18 Gold-Ribbed Hare's Ear. I used a high-sticking technique, working from behind boulders or around logs, to ensure a drag-free drift through some of the faster stretches.

The North Mills River runs right through a nice overnight campground that is generally open year-round but was closed for a construction project when I last visited. Much of the upper creek's wild trout water is tight-quartered, requires stealth, and does not offer much room for a back cast. Trace Ridge Trailhead near the campground offers a network of paths that is popular with hikers and trail riders as well as anglers. Hendersonville Reservoir is a serene little watershed dam that marks the beginning of the North Mills at the junction of Big and Fletcher Creeks. Primitive camping is allowed in designated backcountry areas. This wild and beautiful area is a nice alternative to the more heavily fished Davidson River.

The North Mills Recreation Area is easy to find. Located between Asheville and Brevard, it is not far from the town of Fletcher, home to the annual Western North Carolina Fly Fishing Expo. Heading east (physically, southeast) out of Asheville on I-26, take exit 40 near the Asheville Regional Airport and head west onto Highway 280 (Boylston Highway). Turn right at the first traffic light past the Highway 191 intersection onto North Mills River Road. Travel north about 5 miles to the recreation area.

Does a bear sit in the woods? This one did, about 90 yards distant from the stream, and watched me while she and her cubs fed on remnant corn.

Types of Fish
Rainbow trout, brown trout, and brook trout.

Known Hatches
Baetis, Black Caddis, Black Stonefly, Blue Quill, Blue-Winged Olive, Cream Midge, Gray Caddis, Gray Fox, Green Drake, Hendrickson, Isonychia, Light Cahill, March Brown, midge, Quill Gordon, Giant Stonefly, terrestrials, Yellow Midge, Yellow Stonefly.

Equipment to Use
Rods: 3- to 5-weight, 8 to 9 feet in length.
Reels: Standard.
Lines: Floating to match rod length.
Leaders: 5x to 7x, 9 to 14 feet in length.

Flies to Use
Drys: Adams, sizes 16-18; Black Beetle, 14-16; Blue Thorax Dun, 18-22; Blue-Winged Olive Parachute, 14-20; Blue Quill, 14-18; Cahill, 14-20; Coffin Fly, 14-18; Dave's Hopper, 12-14; Elk-Hair Caddis, 16-18; Flying Ant, 12-18; Griffith's Glo Bug, 14-18; Gnat, 20; Gray Midge, 18-22; Hendrickson, 14-18; Humpy, 16-18; Inchworm, 14-18; Irresistible, 14-18; Little Yellow Sally, 14-20; March Brown, 16-18; Mosquito, 14-18; Quill Gordon, 12-20; Royal Coachman, 14-18; Royal Wulff, 14-18; Stimulator, 12-18; Thunderhead, 12-16; Yellow Hammer, 10-14.

Nymphs & Streamers: Brassie, sizes 14-18; Beadhead Pheasant Tail Nymph, 16-18; Beadhead Gold-Ribbed Hare's Ear, 14-16; Bullethead Grasshopper, 10; Copper John, 14-18; Damsel, 14-16; Flashback Hare's Ear Nymph, 14-18; Gray Ghost, 8-12; Little Prince Nymph, 16-18; March Brown Nymph, 16-18; Mickey Finn, 8-10; Muddler Minnow, 6-10; Pat's Nymph;, 18-24; San Juan Worm, 14-16; Scud, 12-18; Sculpin, 6-8; Stone Nymph, 6-10; Woolly Bugger, 6-10.

When to Fish
Fall and spring are the best times to fish here.

Season & Limits
The delayed-harvest season runs from October 1 through June 1 and the river is stocked monthly during this season.

Nearby Fly Fishing
The Davidson River is just down the road on the way to Brevard. The South Mills River, near the Cradle of Forestry Historic Area located just off of Highway 276, is home to wild brown trout with no closed season. Fire Service Road 476, below the gauging, station is another good place on the South Mills to explore for wild trout.

Accommodations & Services
The cities of Asheville and Brevard are within an hour of the North Mills River.

Helpful Website
www.davidsonflyfishing.com

Rating
The North Mills rates an 8.

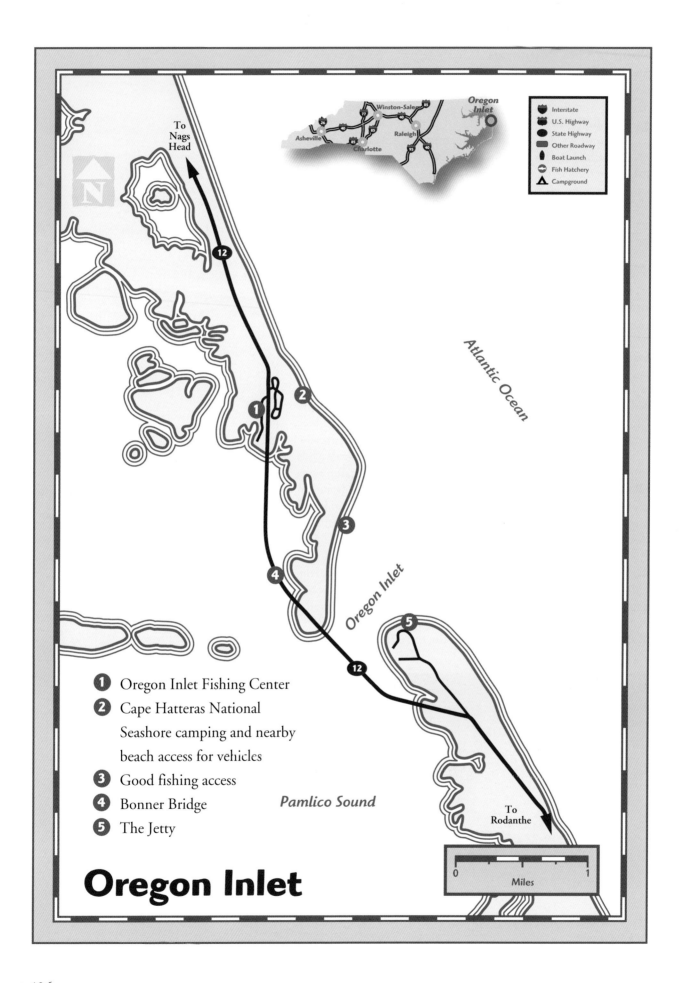

Map Legend

- Interstate
- U.S. Highway
- State Highway
- Other Roadway
- Boat Launch
- Fish Hatchery
- Campground

Oregon Inlet

To Nags Head

Atlantic Ocean

Oregon Inlet

Pamlico Sound

To Rodanthe

1 Oregon Inlet Fishing Center
2 Cape Hatteras National
   Seashore camping and nearby
   beach access for vehicles
3 Good fishing access
4 Bonner Bridge
5 The Jetty

Winston-Salem

Asheville

Charlotte

Raleigh

0 Miles 1

Oregon Inlet

Oregon Inlet

When I think of the Outer Banks, Oregon Inlet usually comes to mind. This is a world-class destination for both boat and beach anglers. Some of my favorite memories of fishing with my dad and brother are rooted here. We would cast for drum and blues in the surf, and flounder in the deep channel under the Bonner Bridge that connects the northern Outer Banks to Hatteras Island. Oregon Inlet is named after the side-wheel steamer, Oregon, which was the first vessel to pass between Bodie Island and Pea Island after a powerful hurricane divided the two in 1846.

For the fly fisher, the northern side of the inlet provides easy access to deeper water just a cast away—and it's good when the blues are running in the fall. Off-road vehicles can access portions of the beach. Consult the National Park Service current access maps. The northside beach is closed to all traffic from mid-March through mid-September due to nesting birds. Fall is the best time to fish, when chopper blues come through with sea trout and some

The business end of an Atlantic cutlassfish, also known as a ribbonfish or silver eel. Some anglers use these toothy creatures as bait for king mackerel.

The author fishes the calm waters on the Hatteras Island side of the Oregon Inlet jetty. Photo by Elizabeth Larson.

*Joseph Corso attacks the surf for aggresive bluefish on the
north point at Oregon Inlet on the Outer Banks.*

big drum. Oregon Inlet attracts numerous surf fishers who simply back their vehicles to the beach tide line and have at it. Nearby Oregon Inlet Campground is run by the National Park Service and is a convenient base for serious anglers as well as non-fishing family members.

Across the inlet on the southern side, the jetty provides another opportunity for the fly fisher. And you never know what to expect. One summer afternoon after a long series of casts with a sinking-tip line, I landed a prehistoric eel-like creature with a mouthful of vicious-looking canines. Asking around, I learned that my silvery catch was officially deemed an Atlantic cutlassfish, more commonly referred to as a ribbonfish. An 8-weight is usually my first choice for the jetty, and there is plenty of room for a backcast. Just be aware and watch out for other anglers.

The blue-ribbon waters around Oregon Inlet have produced a good variety of fish that top the North Carolina state records. The record-setting species range across the angling spectrum and include a 5-pound croaker, a 744-pound bluefin tuna, a 768-pound mako shark, and a 1,142-pound blue marlin.

A kayak is another great way to test these waters. If you paddle, always be aware of fast-moving boat traffic. A few Novembers ago, a friend took me out in his fishing boat but his GPS was on the fritz, so we had to be sure and maintain visual contact with the Bonner Bridge. We were targeting stripers, also known here as rockfish. Right about the time we started marking fish, the motor sputtered out. The depth finder still worked, so I could see the shrinking depths as we drifted toward dangerous shoals. The gauge reading changed from 12 feet to 6 pretty quickly. Then the fog rolled in, and we lost all sight of the bridge. Fortunately our skipper and his first mate managed to re-start the motor, and we found our way back safely. That Thanksgiving on the Outer Banks I gave sincere thanks and shook my head in wonder. I left with a more profound appreciation for those who brave the volatile conditions off North Carolina's Outer Banks, which are often referred to as the "Graveyard of the Atlantic."

A view from the beach just north of Oregon Inlet. This section of beach is closed each spring to protect the nesting activity of birds, including piping plovers, terns, and black skimmers.

The jetty at Oregon Inlet offers ample opportunity for the fly fisher. Caution here, those rocks can be quite slippery and watch out for other anglers with your back cast. Watch the water for rogue waves and the wakes of large fishing boats.

Types of Fish

Bluefish, red drum, flounder, speckled trout, gray trout, croaker, Spanish mackerel, stripers, and cobia.

Known Baitfish

Anglers at Oregon Inlet can expect finger mullet, menhaden, shrimp, squid, ribbonfish, crabs, and other small baitfish.

Equipment to Use

Rods: 6- to 9-weight rods, 9 to 9½ feet in length.
Reels: Mechanical and large-arbor reels.
Lines: Intermediate floating line, 10- to 15-foot sinking-tip lines for sea trout.
Leaders: 0x to 2x leaders, 9 feet in length (wire leaders should be used for bluefish).
Wading: Anglers can use chest waders, wet wade, or use kayaks or larger boats.

Flies to Use

Bend Back, sizes 1/0-2; Bruce's Crystal Shrimp, 1/0; Clouser Minnow, 2/0-4; DuBiel's Finesse Fly, 2-4; DuBiel's Lil'Hadden, 1/0-2; DuBiel's Red-Ducer, 1/0-2; Lefty's Deceiver, 2/0-2; Lefty's Half & Half, 2/0-2; Popovics's Surf Candy, 1/0; Tommy's Crease Fly, 2/0-2; Tommy's Eel Fly, 2/0 and 1/0; Trow's Minnow, 3/0-6; Wirt's Redfish Rattler, 2/0-2.

When to Fish

Spring and fall are the best times to fish, but summer and winter can produce good angling as well.

Season & Limits

Open all year. Consult a copy of the current North Carolina regulations for the species and season.

Nearby Fly Fishing

Bodie Island Lighthouse area. Various channels, islands, and sloughs on the sound side of Hatteras National Seashore.

Accommodations & Services

Oregon Inlet Fishing Center across from the campground, just north of the inlet on N.C. 12, is close and offers every resource for an angler.

Rating

This is a favorite destination and rates a 9.

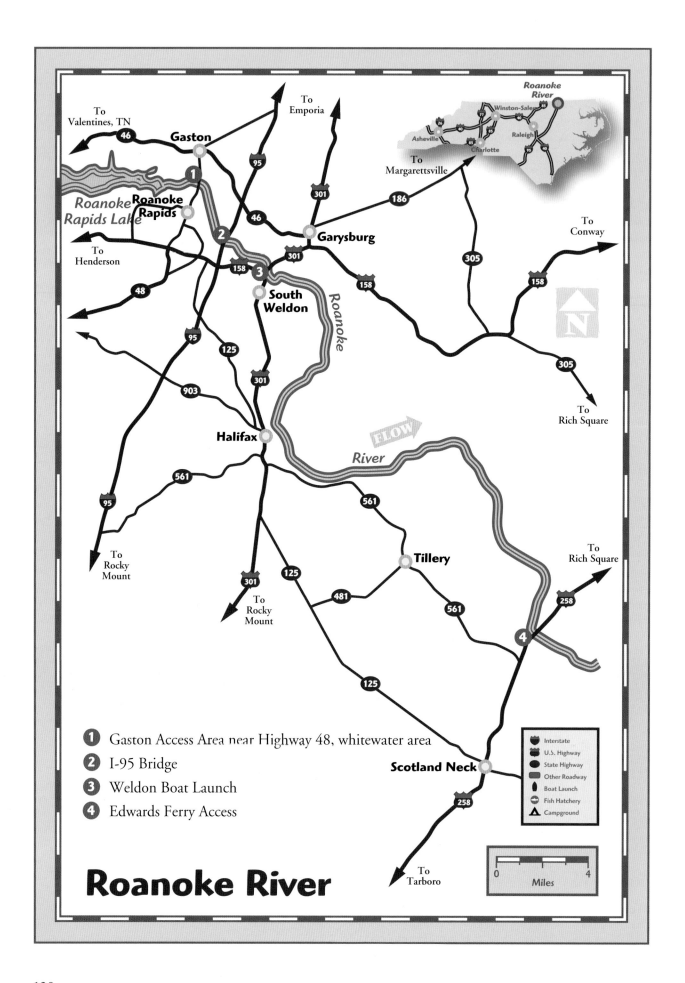

To Valentines, TN

To Emporia

Gaston

46

95

Roanoke Rapids Lake **Roanoke Rapids**

Roanoke River

To Margarettsville

186

To Conway

301

46

Garysburg

301

158

305

158

To Henderson

158

48

South Weldon

95

125

903

301

Halifax

561

95

561

Tillery

125

481

561

258

To Rocky Mount

301

To Rocky Mount

FLOW

River

305

To Rich Square

To Rich Square

258

Scotland Neck

258

125

To Tarboro

❶ Gaston Access Area near Highway 48, whitewater area

❷ I-95 Bridge

❸ Weldon Boat Launch

❹ Edwards Ferry Access

🛣	Interstate
🛣	U.S. Highway
🛣	State Highway
▬	Other Roadway
🚤	Boat Launch
⬭	Fish Hatchery
▲	Campground

0 Miles 4

Roanoke River

Roanoke River

Detail of a Roanoke River striper. Photo by Elizabeth Larson.

Roanoke Rapids is named after the rough-and-rocky whitewater in sections of the Roanoke River above Weldon.

North Carolina's Amazon is the way one fellow described the Roanoke River.

Rich with wildlife and a revitalized abundance of anadromous fish, the Roanoke is a revered destination for anglers. Each spring, fishermen from all over congregate on the river near the little town of Weldon in Eastern North Carolina. Weldon is a suburb of Roanoke Rapids and touts itself as the Striper Capital of the World. The fishermen come to this small town for the run of shad that is soon followed by migrating striped bass. Hickory shad are chrome-bright, sea-run fish that act like small tarpon and resemble baby silver kings from their snouts down to their forked tails. They migrate up from the coastal waters of the Albemarle Sound and are followed by a striper run that reaches the upper river in early April and continues through May. Together, the shad and stripers produce some of the most bountiful angling in the Southeast. Improved management practices, such as slot limits and limited

Mike Perry displays his catch. A good raft is essential for chasing shad on the upper Roanoke River, where the rocks can take a toll on canoes or boats made of other materials.

harvests that began in the late 1980s, have turned this fishery into a continuing success story.

Leaps and Bounds

The first time I ever ventured to Roanoke River in search of shad, guide Capt. Gordon Churchill said, "This will make up for any and all fishless days you've ever had." On that memorable day (at the invitation of my fishing buddy Mike Perry) we put in upstream of Weldon and rafted down drift-boat style. Along the way we stopped, anchored, and waded among large boulders. The rafts gave us access to areas of the river that are seldom waded, and we cast to remote waters and felt like we had the river to ourselves. For the Weldon area, where most anglers ply the calm water below the rapids either from boats or the banks, our type of mobile angling would be considered unconventional. It's a little more work, but solitude has its rewards.

Indeed, we pushed the raft out into the rush of clear water and immediately caught flashing glimpses of shad as they scurried from the approaching raft. The tackle was basic, 5-weight fly rods, 9-foot leaders and weighted pink shad darts. Shad darts are very simple small flies with big silver or gold eyes made of bead chain or a cone head. They are usually very colorful, even fluorescent, and contain some extra sparkle in their tail and wing/hackle. Our downstream casts brought fast-and-furious action, and the shad entertained us with acrobatic leaps and line-zipping runs.

Going Deep for Stripers

Following the shad run each spring, the male stripers precede the females and work their way up the Roanoke. These fish are predominately in the 2-pound, 20-inch range. The females are bigger. To catch the stripers, you generally must present your fly just off the bottom. This requires Type IV full-sinking lines or a fast-sinking 30-foot head. An 8-weight 9-foot rod is ideal with a size 2 chartreuse Clouser Minnow or Lefty's Deceiver tied onto a stout 1x or 3x leader. If you are planning your first trip to the Roanoke River, it is a wise idea to enlist the services of a knowledgeable fly-fishing guide who has a boat and who can educate you about the river current, hazards, and the specialized fly-fishing techniques required for chasing stripers on this river.

Topwater Tails

When the water temperatures warm to the upper 60s, the surface action heats up. The best times for landing a surface-caught striper are within an hour or two of dawn and dusk. A medium popping bug stripped fast, loudly, and splashy will catch the attention of frenzied males that are often milting, chasing females, and traveling in schools of up to 20 or more. According to guide Capt. Dean Lamont, the larger females come to the top, the males follow them up, bump them and knock out the eggs, and then fertilize the floating eggs. Being out on the river surrounded by milky clouds of mating stripers is a surreal and unforgettable experience.

A selection of colorful striper flies for the Roanoke River.

Types of Fish

Striped bass, hickory shad, American shad, catfish, and largemouth bass.

Known Hatches

The forage here includes river herring, crustaceans, smaller fish, and frogs.

Equipment to Use

Rods: An 8-weight is ideal for stripers. 5- to 6-weights are fine for shad.
Reels: Mechanical and large arbor reels. A disc drag will help with stripers.
Lines: Floating lines for topwater, otherwise, fast to intermediate sinking-tip lines matched to rod. Also 200- to 400-grain sinking-tip lines.
Leaders: 1x through 4x, 9 feet in length for shad and topwater. Use shorter 3- to 4-foot leaders for sinking lines.
Wading: Bring chest waders for when you have to get out of the boat or fish from the rocks.

Flies to Use

Surface: Blados's Crease Fly, size 4; DP Popper, 4-6; DP Slider, 2-4; Walt's Saltwater Popper, chartreuse, 2-8; Wilkins's Fire Tiger Bass Popper, 4-6.
Subsurface: Chocklett's Gummy Minnow, sizes 4-6; Clouser Minnow, 1/0-6; Cowen's Baitfish, 2-6; Crazy Charlie, 4-6; Krystal Bugger, 1/a0-6; Lefty's Deceiver, 2/0-6; Muddler Minnow, 2-8; Shad Dart, 4-8; Woolly Bugger, 2-8.

When to Fish

Spring fishing begins with the shad run followed by the stripers. Explore the lower river in the fall, fish for largemouth bass, camp, and enjoy the wilderness experience.

Season & Limits

Much of the reason for the success of this fishery is due to the strictly enforced size and daily creel limits. The season for striped bass is currently March 1 to April 30. There is an 18-inch minimum and no fish can be held between 22-27 inches. Only two can be held, including only one greater than 27 inches. There are fewer shad restrictions, as they are not often kept. For further details consult a current edition of the North Carolina Wildlife Resources Commission Regulations Digest or find it online at www.ncwildlife.org.

Nearby Fly Fishing

Lake Gaston, Chowan River, and Merchants Millpond.

Accommodations & Services

Roanoke Rapids is the biggest nearby town and offers a variety of lodging and supplies.

Rating

This river offers so much, it rates a solid 9.

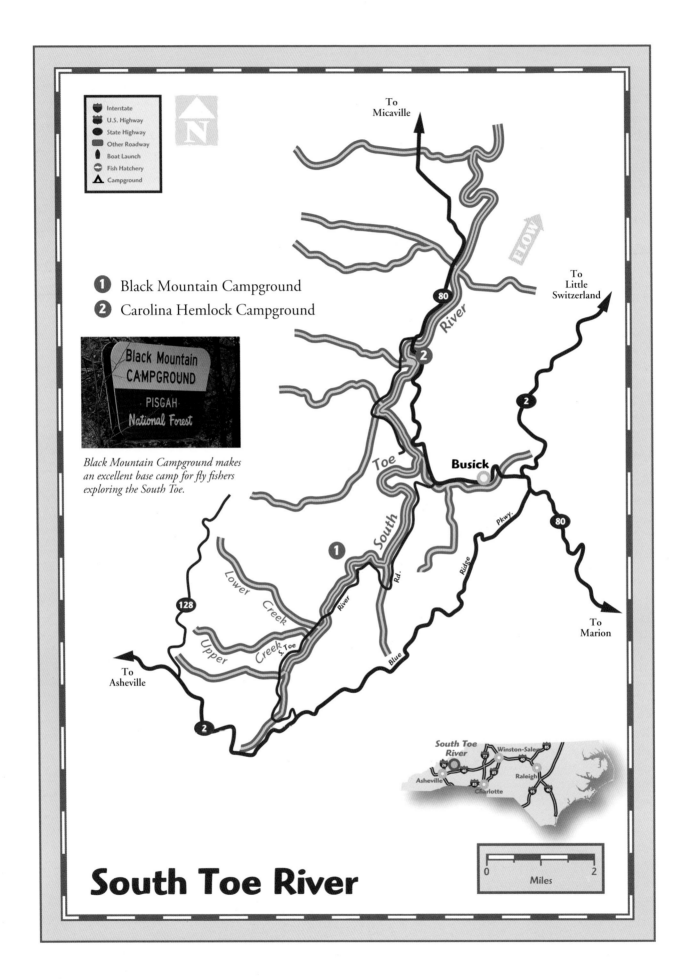

Legend:
- Interstate
- U.S. Highway
- State Highway
- Other Roadway
- Boat Launch
- Fish Hatchery
- Campground

N

To Micaville

To Little Switzerland

FLOW

1 Black Mountain Campground
2 Carolina Hemlock Campground

Black Mountain CAMPGROUND PISGAH National Forest

Black Mountain Campground makes an excellent base camp for fly fishers exploring the South Toe.

80

River

2

Toe

Busick

South

2

Ridge Pkwy.

80

River Rd.

128

Lower Creek

Upper Creek

S. Toe

Blue

To Asheville

2

To Marion

South Toe River

Winston-Salem

Asheville

Raleigh

Charlotte

0   Miles   2

South Toe River

South Toe River

A colorful fly-caught, wild brown from the middle section of the South Toe.

Yellow foliage still framed the streamside in the last days of October, but autumn felt warm, and the mild weather made for comfortable days in the mountains. Still, the Yancey County nights were cold at my streamside camp, and there was always the potential of being rousted by a voracious bruin. With bears in mind, I took care to put food away in my vehicle and to not eat or cook where I slept.

I camped in the shadow of Mount Mitchell, which, at 6,684 feet, is the highest point in the U.S. east of the Mississippi River. The campsite and the mountain are just a short, rugged drive from the beloved Blue Ridge Parkway within the Pisgah National Forest.

The South Toe is a small, classic freestone mountain stream. There are upper, middle, and lower sections. The "Wild Trout" upper section is typical of many mountain headwaters: tight quarters with gnarly rhododendron guarding the native brook trout. There is no closed season, with a daily limit of four fish and

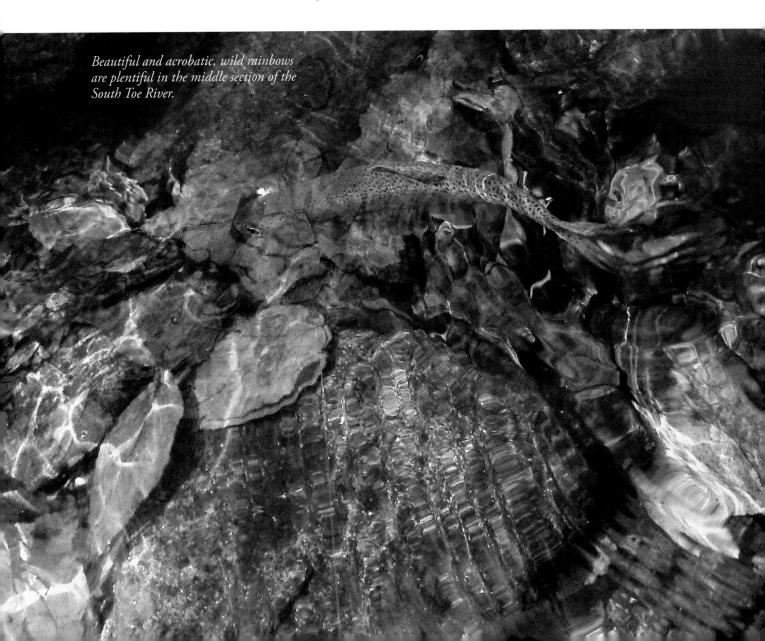

Beautiful and acrobatic, wild rainbows are plentiful in the middle section of the South Toe River.

The lower section of the South Toe flows past Carolina Hemlock campground (wooded area on the left).

a minimum size of seven inches. A nearby feeder stream worth checking out is the crystalline catch-and-release water of Upper Creek, near the Blue Ridge Parkway.

Small but Feisty

A 3-weight fly rod proved ideal for the brightly colored wild rainbows and browns that inhabit the gin-clear waters of the middle section, which is catch-and-release and fly-fishing-only. Generally, this is the preferred section for fly fishers, and it is adjacent to Black Mountain Campground. These fish are small, averaging only 6 through 10 inches with occasional exceptions, but they are wild and make up for their size with robust leaping ability. Much of the middle section of the Toe features shallow runs and good access with some surprisingly deep pools. You just know there are bigger fish lurking around the next bend. The key roads are South Toe River Road, which follows much of the river, and Highway 80 that will get you in and out.

On the drive down to the lower section of the river I passed the other public campground, Carolina Hemlock, and on the same route, was impressed by the splendor of Mount Mitchell Golf Course. The lower South Toe has the character of a larger stream with deeper pools and much higher banks. The campground provides good access to the lower section. This section is much less regulated, allowing bait and no size restrictions. It is hatchery stocked from Clear Creek downstream for eight miles to Yancey County Recreation Park. During warmer months, anglers can catch smallmouth bass or sunfish in addition to trout.

The author examines his fly box on a scenic stretch of the middle section of the South Toe River.

Types of Fish
Brown trout, rainbow trout, and brook trout.

Known Hatches
Baetis, Black Caddis, Black Stonefly, Blue Quill, Blue-Winged Olive, Cream Midge, Gray Caddis, Gray Fox, Green Drake, Hendrickson, Isonychia, Light Cahill, March Brown, midge, Quill Gordon, Giant Stonefly, terrestrials, Yellow Midge, Yellow Stonefly.

Equipment to Use
Rods: 3- to 4-weight for nymphs and dry flies, 5-weight for streamers, all 6 to 8½ feet in length due to tight quarters.
Reels: Any mechanical reel.
Lines: Floating lines to match rod weight.
Leaders: 9- to 12-foot leaders tapered to 4x or 6x.
Wading: Chest waders are recommended due to the deeper pools.

Flies to Use
Drys: Adams, sizes 16-18; Black Beetle, 14-16; Blue Thorax Dun, 18-22; Blue-Winged Olive Parachute, 14-20; Blue Quill, 14-18; Cahill, 14-20; Coffin Fly, 14-18; Dave's Hopper, 12-14; Elk-Hair Caddis, 16-18; Flying Ant, 12-18; Griffith's Glo Bug, 14-18; Gnat, 20; Gray Midge, 18-22; Hendrickson, 14-18; Humpy, 16-18; Inchworm, 14-18; Irresistible, 14-18; Little Yellow Sally, 14-20; March Brown, 16-18; Mosquito, 14-18; Quill Gordon, 12-20; Royal Coachman, 14-18; Royal Wulff, 14-18; Stimulator, 12-18; Thunderhead, 12-16; Yellow Hammer, 10-14.

Nymphs & Streamers: Brassie, sizes 14-18; Beadhead Pheasant Tail Nymph, 16-18; Beadhead Gold-Ribbed Hare's Ear Nymph, 14-16; Bullethead Grasshopper, 10; Copper John, 14-18; Damsel, 14-16; Flashback Hare's Ear Nymph, 14-18; Gray Ghost, 8-12; Little Prince Nymph, 16-18; March Brown Nymph, 16-18; Mickey Finn, 8-10; Muddler Minnow, 6-10; Pat's Nymph, 18-24; San Juan Worm, 14-16; Scud, 12-18; Sculpin, 6-8; Stone Nymph, 6-10; Woolly Bugger, 6-10.

When to Fish
Spring and fall are ideal. Water levels are lower during summer months.

Season & Limits
The middle section of the South Toe is open year-round, and fishing is single-hook artificial flies and catch-and-release-only. All the streams are well marked with diamond-shaped signs.

Nearby Fly Fishing
The North Toe River and Nolichucky River.

Accommodations and Services
The towns of Burnsville and Busick offer limited amenities. Carolina Hemlock and Black Mountain Campground offer first-come, first-served tent and trailer fee camping. Primitive sites in Pisgah National Forest along the road are marked with brown signs.

Helpful Web Sites
www.forestcamping.com/dow/southern/pisgcmp.htm

Rating
Beautiful in the fall and fun to explore, I rate the South Toe an 8.

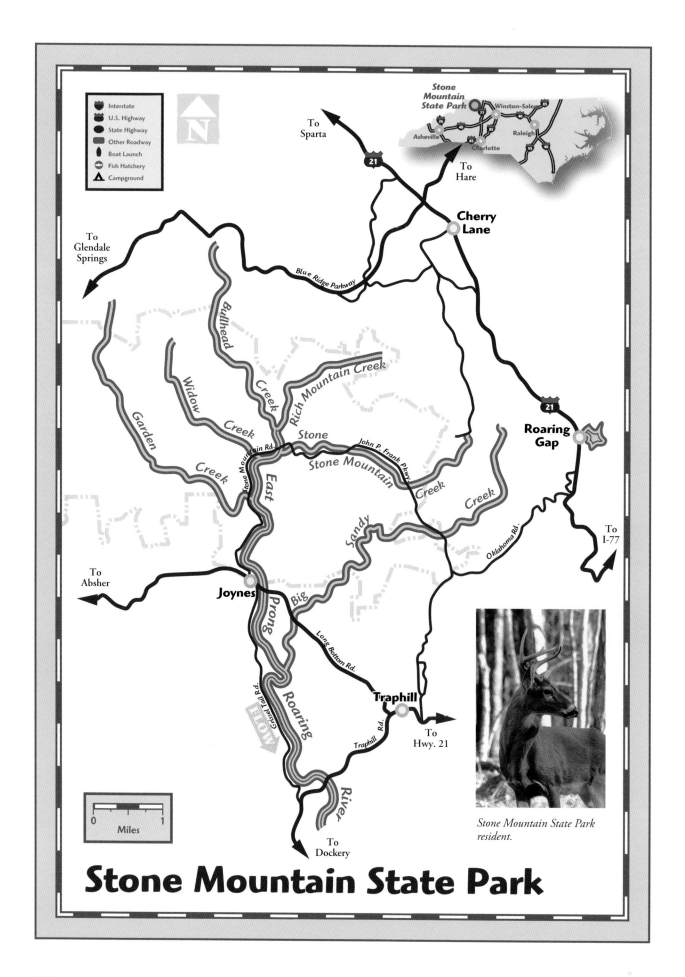

Legend

- Interstate
- U.S. Highway
- State Highway
- Other Roadway
- Boat Launch
- Fish Hatchery
- Campground

To Sparta

Stone Mountain State Park

Winston-Salem

Asheville

Raleigh

Charlotte

To Hare

Cherry Lane

Blue Ridge Parkway

To Glendale Springs

Bullhead Creek

Rich Mountain Creek

Widow Creek

Garden Creek

Stone

Stone Mountain Rd.

John P. Frank Pkwy.

Roaring Gap

Stone Mountain

East

Sandy

Creek

Creek

Oklahoma Rd.

To I-77

To Absher

Joynes

Big

Prong

Long Bottom Rd.

Grissel Trail Rd.

Roaring

Traphill

Traphill Rd.

To Hwy. 21

River

To Dockery

0   1
Miles

Stone Mountain State Park resident.

Stone Mountain State Park

138

Stone Mountain State Park

Stone Mountain State Park is a must-visit destination for those who have never been or are new to the state. Located just off the Blue Ridge Parkway between Elkin and Sparta, this natural wonderland boasts more than 20 miles of trout streams. Sprawling across 14,000 acres over Alleghany and Wilkes counties, Stone Mountain was named after the 600-foot granite rock face that towers over everything in the vicinity. Stone Mountain Creek flows beside the main park road and eventually morphs into the East Prong of the Roaring River. It is a delayed-harvest stocked stream that has undergone immense renovation. This medium-sized river starts off small, flowing fast and gradually decreasing speed into slower runs and pools at the outer edge of the park. The prolific evergreen rhododendrons shroud much of the interior and create a jungle-like environment. Stealth and excellent roll casting skills are required on the smaller streams designated Wild Trout Waters.

This 25-inch brown stalked the Bullhead Creek section of Stone Mountain State Park. Photo by Jeff Wilkins.

The author probes Stone Mountain Creek. Photo by Elizabeth Larson.

Angler on the East Prong of the Roaring River. Photo by Elizabeth Larson.

These are well marked just off the main road and include Garden Creek, Widow Creek, and Big Sandy Creek.

There are plenty of trout and good access for the handicapped. Anglers take note, it can get crowded during warmer weather, especially on weekends. I recommend spring, fall, and winter trips to avoid crowds. There is also a nice campground, open year-round, plenty of hiking trails, rock climbing, and 200-foot waterfalls to explore. Under the right conditions, this can be one of the best places to observe deer, turkeys, or even the occasional rare glimpse of an otter or bobcat.

A unique feature within the park is Bullhead Creek, a pay-to-play, catch-and-release stream that was once the domain of the Blue Ridge Fly Fishers. This classic freestone water is an old fashioned English-style beat stream with eight sections reserved for anglers who may sign up for a specific beat to fish all day. The cost is $22 per angler, per beat per day. You must self-register at the parking area. The beats are first-come, first-served. Beat 3 is actually Rich Mountain Creek, tributary to Bullhead, a smaller stream with more normal-sized trout. Bullhead Creek, however, has some trophy wild trout that grow big from pellet feedings by park personnel. This stream requires a fishing net and barbless hooks. No pellet imitation flies are allowed.

No matter what your level of expertise, Stone Mountain State Park can offer a unique fly-fishing challenge. The wildlife and beauty of the surroundings enhance the angling experience. To get there from I-77 heading north, take exit #83/ HWY 21 North/ Sparta/Roaring Gap (exit from the left lane). Travel north about 13 miles to Traphill Road/ (SR 1002) You will see a brown sign for the park. Turn left and go 4 miles to the next brown sign. Turn right onto the John P. Frank Parkway that leads into the park.

From North Wilkesboro take N.C. 18 north, then turn right onto HWY 268 East. Go about 3 miles and turn left at Airport Road. Go about 4 miles and turn left. This becomes Traphill Road, (SR 1002). Follow the road to the John P. Frank Parkway (SR 1784) and turn left, following the parkway to the park.

A wintry view of Rich Mountain Creek, Beat 3.

Types of Fish
Rainbow trout, brown trout, and brook trout.

Known Hatches
Baetis, Black Caddis, Black Stonefly, Blue Quill, Blue-Winged Olive, Cream Midge, Gray Caddis, Gray Fox, Green Drake, Hendrickson, Isonychia, Light Cahill, March Brown, midge, Quill Gordon, Giant Stonefly, Sulfur, terrestrials, Yellow Midge, and Yellow Stonefly.

Equipment to Use
Rods: 3- to 5-weight, 7 to 9 feet in length.
Reels: Standard mechanical.
Lines: Weight-forward floating, matched to rod.
Leaders: 5x through 7x leaders, 9 feet in length.
Wading: Hip waders are fine here.

Flies To Use
Drys: Adams, sizes 16-20; Black Beetle, 14-16; Blue-Winged Olive Parachute, 14-20; Blue Quill, 14-18; Cahill, 14-20; Coffin Fly, 14-18; Dave's Hopper, 12-14; Elk-Hair Caddis, 16-18; Flying Ant, 12-18; Griffith's Glo Bug, 14-18; Gnat, 20; Hendrickson, 14-18; Humpy, 16-18; Inchworm, 14-18; Irresistible, 14-18; Little Yellow Sally, 14-20; March Brown, 16-18; Mosquito, 14-18; Quill Gordon, 12-20; Royal Coachman, 14-18; Royal Wulff, 14-18; Stimulator, 12-18.
Nymphs & Streamers: Brassie, sizes 14-18; Beadhead Pheasant Tail Nymph, 16-18; Beadhead Gold-Ribbed Hare's Ear Nymph, 14-16; Copper John, 14-18; Damsel, 14-16; Flashback Hare's Ear Nymph, 14-18; Little Prince Nymph, 16-18; March Brown Nymph, 16-18; Mickey Finn, 8-10; Muddler Minnow, 6-10; Pat's Nymph, 18-24; San Juan Worm, 14-16; Scud, 12-18; Sculpin, 6-8; Stone Nymph, 6-10; Woolly Bugger, 6-10.

When to Fish
Avoid summer due to low water and big crowds. March through May is decent as are the fall months. Winter can offer solitude but watch the temperature as your rod guides may freeze up.

Seasons & Limits
Fishing is permitted year-round, from 8 a.m. until one hour before the park closes.

Big Sandy Creek, Stone Mountain Creek (Alleghany County Section), Widow Creek, and Garden Creek are designated Wild or Native Streams. Any rod and reel may be used, single hook artificial lures only. 4 trout may be kept per person, per day, over seven inches long. Bullhead and Rich Mountain Creek are catch and release streams. They require a fly rod, barbless fly hooks, a fishing net and a daily fee. Stone Mountain Creek (Wilkes County) and Roaring Fork, East Prong in Stone Mountain State Park are Delayed Harvest Streams. From the first day of October through the first Saturday in June, no trout may be harvested or possessed. Fishing is restricted to artificial lures having one single hook. From the first Saturday in June through the last day of September, you may use any bait and any lure. You may keep up to seven fish, no size limit.

Nearby Fly Fishing
Blue Ridge Parkway is nearby as well as the New River just to the north of Sparta.

Accommodations & Services
Stone Mountain State Park Campground: (336) 957-8185 is seven miles southwest of Roaring Gap and 25 miles northeast of North Wilkesboro. The town of Elkin is just southeast of the park on U.S. 21 and also offers some basic amenities.

Rating
With an interesting variety of water to fish, I rate Stone Mountain Park an 8.

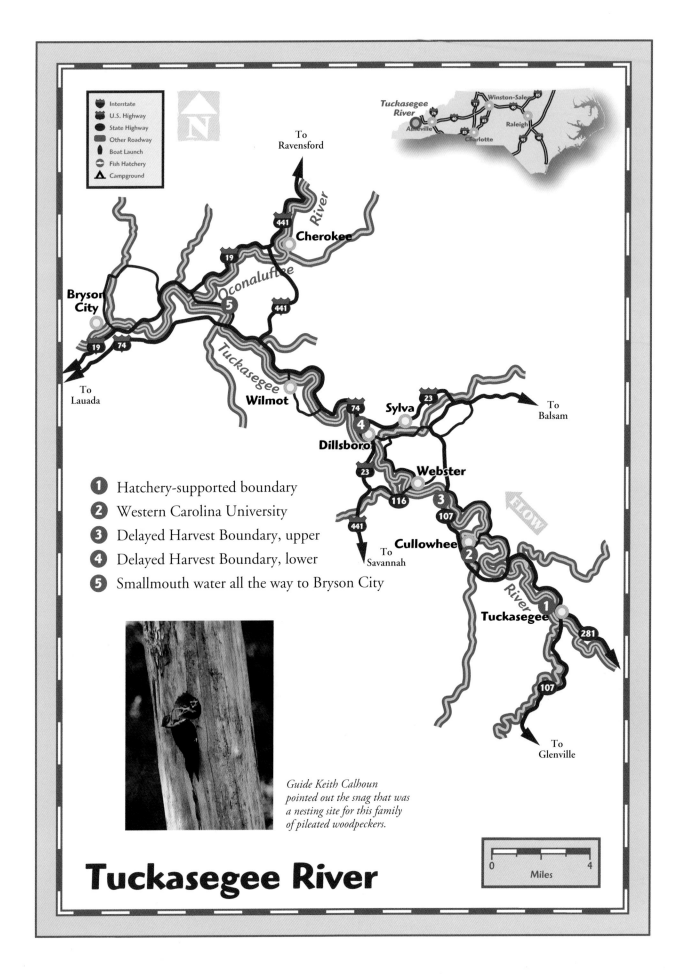

Legend:
- Interstate
- U.S. Highway
- State Highway
- Other Roadway
- Boat Launch
- Fish Hatchery
- Campground

N

Tuckasegee River
Asheville
Winston-Salem
Charlotte
Raleigh

To Ravensford

Cherokee

Oconaluftee River

Bryson City

To Lauada

Tuckasegee

Wilmot

Sylva

To Balsam

Dillsboro

Webster

To Savannah

Cullowhee

FLOW

Tuckasegee River

To Glenville

1. Hatchery-supported boundary
2. Western Carolina University
3. Delayed Harvest Boundary, upper
4. Delayed Harvest Boundary, lower
5. Smallmouth water all the way to Bryson City

Guide Keith Calhoun pointed out the snag that was a nesting site for this family of pileated woodpeckers.

0   Miles   4

Tuckasegee River

Tuckasegee River

By North Carolina trout-stream standards, the Tuckasegee River is a large-size tailrace river. Located southwest of Asheville and south of Sylva, The "Tuck" begins in Jackson County where the East and West Forks come together. The river flows northwesterly through Swain County to Bryson City and into the Little Tennessee River section of Fontana Lake. During delayed-harvest season, from October 1 to the first Saturday in June, the upper section near Western Carolina University is said to have more trout per mile than any other river in North Carolina.

My introduction to the Tuckasegee began when I presented a slide show to the Nat Greene Fly Fishers in Greensboro. There, I met boat builder Keith Calhoun after admiring his handcrafted red drift boat out in the parking lot. During our conversation, I learned that he was an experienced Tuckasegee River guide and that he was familiar with *Our Southern Highlanders,* by Horace Kephart, a book that I had mentioned during my presentation. Back in the early 1900s, when the author Kephart first arrived in western North Carolina to write about life in the region, resident Granville Calhoun was the first pioneer to befriend him. Granville had been showcased in a lively chapter about a mountain bear hunt. Keith told me about his ties to the region and that he was indeed kin to Granville.

Types of Fish
There is a good mix of rainbows and brook trout with the occasional brown trout in the delayed-harvest section. The headwaters feature mostly brookies. Near Bryson City, as the water warms, you will encounter a healthy population of bronzebacks.

Known Hatches
Blue Quill, Blue-Winged Olive, Brown Dun, Brown Caddis, Brown Drake, Cream Cahills, Cream Caddis, Damselflies, Dragonflies, Golden Stones, Giant Stoneflies, Gray Fox, Green Drake, Green Rockworm, Green Sedge, Hendrickson, Light Cahill, Little Black Winter Stones, Little Brown Stones, March Browns, midges, Olive Caddis, Quill Gordon, Short-horned Sedge, Sulphurs, terrestrials, Tricos, Yellow Sallies, Willowflies.

Equipment to Use
Rods: 5- to 8-weight, 8 to 9½ feet in length.
Reels: Standard trout reel.
Lines: Weight-forward floating lines matched to rod.
Leaders: 3x to 5x, 9 to 12 feet in length.
Wading: You will surely need waders here and a wading staff wouldn't hurt.

Flies to Use
Drys: Adams, sizes 16-18; Jeff's Beetle, 14-16; Black Caddis, size 10; Blue Thorax Dun, 18-22; Blue-Winged Olive Parachute, 16-20; Blue Quill, 14-18; Cahill, 14-20;

Continued

Brook in the net. This was only an average-size brook trout on the river that boasts more trout per mile than any other North Carolina freshwater stream.

Flip cast. Keith Calhoun maneuvers his hand-crafted drift boat into casting position for Elizabeth Larson.

A few weeks later I found myself in that same drift boat on a fishing trip guided by Calhoun and learned what a beautiful river the Tuck really is. Along the way Calhoun pointed out formations that were remnants of fishing weirs, V-shaped stone structures constructed by Native Americans that were once used to corral and harvest fish including the native species sicklefin, redhorse sucker, and brook trout. We floated through some pastoral farmland and wooded stretches with magnificent mountain vistas that were the ancient home of the Cherokee people. We even watched a pileated woodpecker fly up to a hollow snag tree and feed its young. As we drifted, we took turns casting our fly line rigged with a weighted nymph and a yarn strike indicator. When we found a good hole, Calhoun would drop anchor. We caught and released numerous healthy rainbows and brook trout. The Tuck is known for its prolific caddis hatches. Egg patterns are effective and streamers work when the water is high. One obvious reason the Tuckasegee has been so popular with anglers is because twenty-inch trout are not uncommon.

A five-mile stretch from N.C. Highway 107 in Tuskasegee down to the Dillsboro dam is the most heavily stocked area in the state. One of the challenges to fishing the river is learning to forecast the timing of scheduled flow releases by the Duke Energy–controlled reservoirs. While there are some good places fly fishers can wade, there is private property to avoid. A drift boat with a competent and friendly guide is definitely a fun and productive way to go. There is also some scenic brook-trout water up on the East Tuck near Lake Toxaway. Take N.C. Highway 281 north off U.S. Highway 64 for about a mile. The road bypasses some nice neighborhoods and leads to a parking area. Look for Cold Mountain Road, and take a left just past the Lake Toxaway Fire Station. Continue north on Cold Mountain Road past Lake Toxaway to where it ends. A fire break runs northward to the river. Good topo maps and orienteering skills are highly recommended in this section near Panthertown Valley. The best map of the area can be obtained through www.panthertownmap.com.

Below the delayed-harvest section, beyond the dam all the way to Bryson City, the water begins to warm up. Along this stretch, there are fewer trout, but a nice mixed bag with lots of smallmouth bass, carp, and the occasional walleye or muskie. This area was once the site of the sacred Cherokee village known as Kittowa.

Nice view. An upstream glance back during a Tuckasegee float trip with Keith Calhoun and Elizabeth Larson.

Flies to Use (continued)

Coffin Fly, sizes 14-18; Dave's Hopper, 12-14; Elk-Hair Caddis, 10-14; Flying Ant, 12-18; Griffith's Glo Bug, 14-18; Girdle Bug, 10-12; Gnat, 20; Gray Midge, 18-22; Hendrickson, 14-18; Humpy, 16-18; Inchworm, 14-18; Irresistible, 14-18; Little Yellow Sally, 14-20; March Brown, 16-18; Mosquito, 14-18; October Caddis, 18-20; Quill Gordon, 12-20; Royal Coachman, 14-18; Royal Wulff, 14-18; Stimulator, 12-18; Thunderhead, 12-16; White Mayfly, 10-12; Yellow Hammer, 10-14.

Nymphs & Streamers: Brassie, sizes 14-18; Beadhead Pheasant Tail, 16-18; Beadhead Gold Ribbed Hare's Ear, 14-16; Bullethead Grasshopper, size 10; Copper John, 14-18; Damsel, 14-16; Flashback Hare's Ear, 14-18; Gray Ghost, 8-12; Little Prince Nymph, 16-18; March Brown Nymph, 16-18; Mickey Finn, 8-10; Muddler Minnow, 6-10; Pat's Nymph;, 18-24; San Juan Worm, 14-16; Scud, 12-18; Sculpin, 6-8; Sucker Spawn, 10-12; Stone Nymph, 10-12; Wickham's Nymph, 12-14; Woolly Bugger, 8-12; Y2K, 10-12.

When to Fish

The best time is from October until June.

Season & Limits

See North Carolina Wildlife Resources for Fishing Areas identifying Hatchery Supported, Delayed Harvest, and Wild Trout sections.

Nearby Fly Fishing

Deep Creek, Oconaluftee River, and Nantahala River.

Accommodations & Services

The towns of Dillsboro, Webster, Waynesville, and Sylva offer an abundance of supplies, lodging, and services.

Rating

This is a good river to catch lots of fish and perhaps get "the slam" by catching a 'bow, brown, and brookie. The scenery also makes it special. The Tuck rates a solid 8.

Tuck traffic. A popular river with a dense population of fish, the Tuckasegee attracts many anglers, especially in the spring and fall.

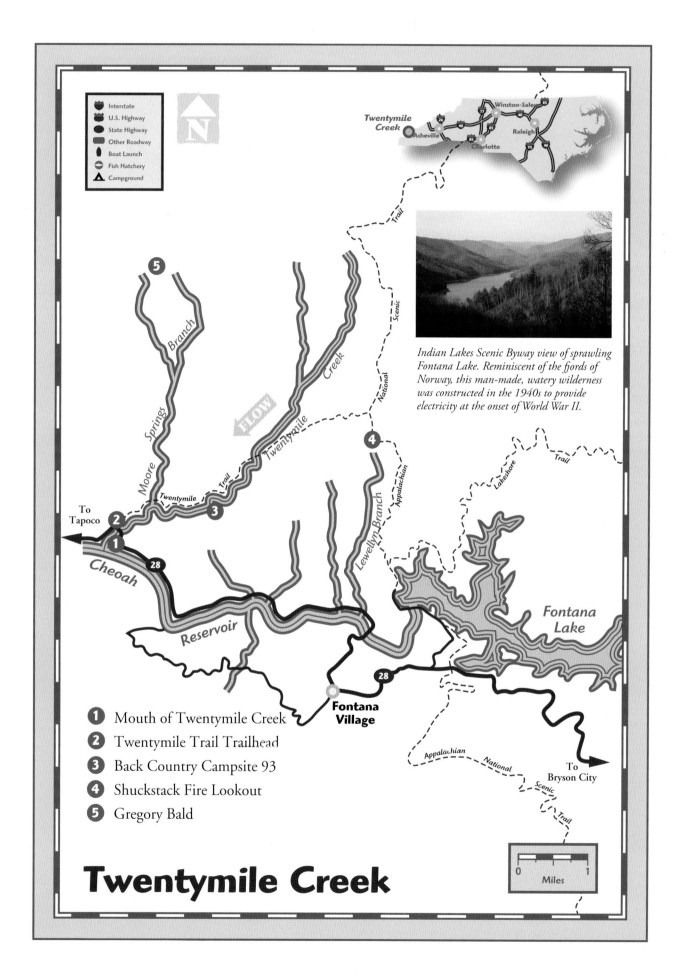

Indian Lakes Scenic Byway view of sprawling Fontana Lake. Reminiscent of the fjords of Norway, this man-made, watery wilderness was constructed in the 1940s to provide electricity at the onset of World War II.

1 Mouth of Twentymile Creek
2 Twentymile Trail Trailhead
3 Back Country Campsite 93
4 Shuckstack Fire Lookout
5 Gregory Bald

Twentymile Creek

Interstate
U.S. Highway
State Highway
Other Roadway
Boat Launch
Fish Hatchery
Campground

Twentymile Creek

Feisty wild rainbow trout inhabit the waters of Twentymile Creek.

The author angling in a small pool on Twentymile Creek.

Dark skies and the threat of heavy rain helped persuade me to investigate this somewhat obscure Smoky Mountain stream. I had been exploring the area around Fontana Lake with the plan of ferrying or backpacking into Hazel Creek. With the storm approaching, I faced the prospect of having to set up camp in the rain. Eventually, the weather grounded me altogether. Fortunately, the Lodge at Fontana Village is a short drive from the lake, and a pleasant night there spared me the displeasure of setting up camp in a downpour. The following morning, with the weather still unsettled, I decided on an alternate day trip. I headed west on N.C. 28 in search of Twentymile Creek.

The drive to the trailhead that leads to the creek is about seven miles from the lodge, and most of it winds by the bucolic Cheoah Reservoir. I found the trailhead just past a small ranger station.

A typical footbridge crossing Twentymile Creek, which is in the southwestern corner of the Smoky Mountains.

The old grade that meanders along the side of the creek offers good access initially. This trail is as popular with backpackers as it is with anglers, although chances are you will have it all to yourself. As you ascend the trail, it becomes a narrow footpath and the stream is more difficult to reach. The banks are often lined with rhododendrons and become gradually steeper. This is where the fly fisher must go "commando," but it usually pays off because the gnarly, jungle-shrouded runs and pools usually contain trout.

As Smoky Mountain National Park streams go, this little gem tends to slip under the radar, and that is precisely what makes it appealing, but if you have time, you may want to check out Twentymile Cascade or the Shuckstack Mountain fire tower. For expansive vistas and colorful azaleas in June, follow the ruggedly steep trail to Gregory Bald on the Tennessee border. Shuckstack and Gregory Bald would require overnight backcountry camping. Backcountry campsite number 93 is only about two miles from the trailhead. It is first come, first served. To camp there you will need a permit. They are free and may be obtained at Fontana Marina. (Twenty Mile Ranger Station is said to have the permits but it was never open when I was there). With more than 2,100 miles of streams and rivers in the Smokies, it is nice to remember that North Carolina and Tennessee have a reciprocal fishing-license agreement.

This medium-sized stream is crisscrossed by numerous primitive log-and-railing footbridges. During my time on Twentymile the water was running high and I learned that the opportunistic wild rainbow trout were eager to accept my invitation. It is said that the stream contains a few secretive browns as well. Moore Springs Branch is the biggest tributary, but not easily fished due to the dense tangle of overhead thickets.

Creepy Crawlers

Sometime later, I learned that Twentymile Creek gets its name not by the length of its course but from the approximate distance between its mouth and the confluence of the old town of Bushnell that was located where the Little Tennessee River met the Tuckasegee River. That confluence is underwater now, flooded by the creation of Fontana Lake. A second explanation has it that the distance was from the creek's confluence to the mouth of Hazel Creek. Regardless of the explanation, Twentymile Creek offers about six miles of walk-in, fishable stream.

As a fly fisher and a wildlife enthusiast, I always enjoy my jaunts into the Smokies. Riparian zones intrigue me. I often look under stones to see what sort of nymphs (trout food) are in the creek. In the Smokies, I often find a colorful little newt instead. The Smoky Mountains are known as the Salamander Capital of the World. There are 30 species of the amphibians here, and they are a sign of a healthy environment. But a note of caution: The Smokies are also home to reptiles, such as northern copperheads and timber rattlers.

In retrospect, I spent a productive afternoon under overcast skies, and I felt fully charged for the challenge ahead: a backpacking odyssey into mythic Hazel Creek.

Types of Fish
Twentymile Creek is known for its frisky rainbows, a few browns, and possibly the occasional brook trout.

Known Hatches
Baetis, Black Caddis, Black Stonefly, Blue Quill, Blue-Winged Olive, Cream Midge, Gray Caddis, Gray Fox, Green Drake, Hendrickson, Isonychia, Light Cahill, March Brown, midge, Quill Gordon, Giant Stonefly, terrestrials, Yellow Midge, Yellow Stonefly.

Equipment to Use
Rods: 3- to 4-weight for nymphs and dry flies, 5-weight for streamers 6 to 8½ feet in length.
Reels: Any mechanical reel.
Lines: Floating lines to match rod weight.
Leaders: 9- to 12-foot leaders tapered to 4x or 6x.
Wading: Chest waders are recommended due to the deeper pools.

Flies to Use
Drys: Adams, sizes 16-18; Black Beetle, 14-16; Blue Thorax Dun, 18-22; Blue-Winged Olive Parachute, 14-20; Blue Quill, 14-18; Cahill, 14-20; Coffin Fly, 14-18; Dave's Hopper, 12-14; Elk-Hair Caddis, 16-18; Flying Ant, 12-18; Griffith's Glo Bug, 14-18; Gnat, 20; Gray Midge, 18-22; Hendrickson, 14-18; Humpy, 16-18; Inchworm, 14-18; Irresistible, 14-18; Little Yellow Sally, 14-20; March Brown, 16-18; Mosquito, 14-18; Quill Gordon, 12-20; Royal Coachman, 14-18; Royal Wulff, 14-18; Sheep Fly, 14-18; Stimulator, 12-18; Thunderhead, 12-16; Yellow Hammer, 10-14.

Nymphs & Streamers: Brassie, sizes 14-18; Beadhead Pheasant Tail Nymph, 16-18; Beadhead Gold-Ribbed Hare's Ear Nymph, 14-16; Bullethead Grasshopper, 10; Copper John, 14-18; Damsel, 14-16; Flashback Hare's Ear Nymph, 14-18; Gray Ghost, 8-12; Little Prince Nymph, 16-18; March Brown Nymph, 16-18; Mickey Finn, 8-10; Muddler Minnow, 6-10; Pat's Nymph; 18-24; San Juan Worm, 14-16; Scud; 12-18; Sculpin, 6-8; Stone Nymph, 6-10; Woolly Bugger, 6-10; Wickham's Nymph, 12-16.

When to Fish
Spring and fall are ideal. Water levels may be lower during summer months.

Season & Limits
Fishing is permitted year-round in areas that are open to fishing.

Nearby Fly Fishing
Eagle Creek, Hazel Creek, and Santeetlah Creek.

Accommodations & Services
The Lodge at Fontana Village, (828) 498-2211, offers a variety of amenities. Great Smoky Mountains National Park requires a permit and advance reservations for backcountry camping in the park. Call (865) 436-1297 for details. The best time to call is from 9 a.m, to 1 p.m. or you can leave a message and have them call you back.

Helpful Web Sites
www.fontanavillage.com
www.yoursmokies.com
www.nps.gov/grsm

Rating
There is a good chance that you may have most of this stream to yourself, for that reason I rate Twentymile Creek an 8.

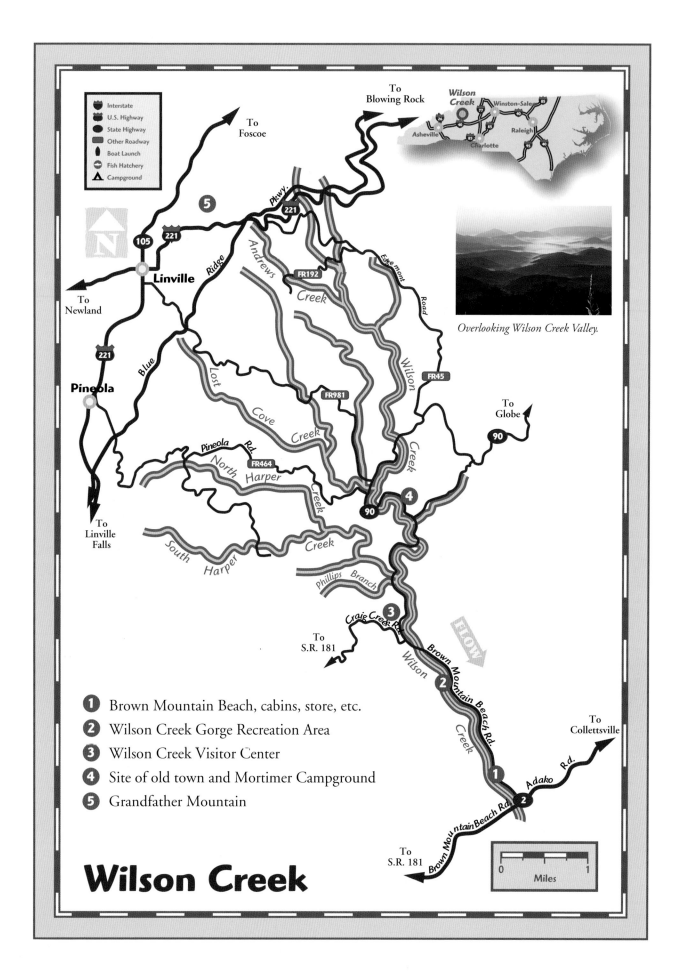

Overlooking Wilson Creek Valley.

1 Brown Mountain Beach, cabins, store, etc.

2 Wilson Creek Gorge Recreation Area

3 Wilson Creek Visitor Center

4 Site of old town and Mortimer Campground

5 Grandfather Mountain

Wilson Creek

Wilson Creek

Scott Cunningham examines a Wilson Creek rainbow trout.

Scott Cunningham and I wound our way up a country road on a crisp winter day heading toward Wilson Creek. Ahead of us, the distinct geometry of Table Rock dominated the skyline. Scott and I swapped fishing stories. He's a young man, but it's evident that he knows a lot about fly fishing. And, as a guide based in nearby Marion, fly fishing is his life. He tells me that there are four distinct sections of Wilson Creek. Those sections consist of the upper Wilson that is catch and release water, wild trout water, a delayed harvest section, and the hatchery-supported section.

Genesis, Chapter I

A tiny spring-fed trickle under the shadow of massive Grandfather Mountain marks the genesis of Wilson Creek. Near the famous Blue Ridge Parkway Viaduct, which overlooks Wilson Creek Valley, you get to see the rugged and wild landscape the creek runs through. Wilson Creek flows for 23 miles before dumping

Lower Wilson Creek Gorge in summer and winter.

Rainbows abound in the delayed-harvest section of Wilson Creek.

into Johns River. From the spring-fed headwaters down to the brawling freestone Wilson Creek Gorge, there is something here for everyone.

As popular with kayakers as it is with anglers, many people associate Wilson Creek with the lower gorge recreation area. During the summer it is not unusual to drive along Brown Mountain Beach Road, and glimpse bikini-clad sun worshippers on the giant rocks below. The huge boulders are reminiscent of Linville Gorge, the neighboring holler just over the ridge. Folks come here to cool off in the deep swimming holes and watch kayakers hone their skills in the whitewater. In summer, it is difficult to find an available turnout or place to park.

During the spring and fall, a fly fisher might want to probe those pools with a weighted streamer in search of brown trout. As you proceed upstream, out of the 2.2-mile gorge area, the next stretch from Phillips Branch to Lost Cove Creek is the delayed-harvest section, home to many a wary rainbow trout. Next is the wild trout water, and finally (marked with diamond-shaped signs), the catch-and-release upper section where the purist can stalk brook trout. If you plan on bushwhacking up around the headwaters, you will need a good map and compass because it gets tricky and steep up near the Blue Ridge Parkway.

Ice Breaker

Winter is a challenging time here for the angler. Small black stoneflies and some blue-winged olives are the only hatches. The landscape is starkly beautiful. Dagger-like icicles cling to canyon walls. Patches of snow blanket the shadows. White sycamore tree limbs reach to the sky like so many arms.

Scott Cunningham's recent clients here included a nine-year-old boy and his parents. He tells me that two days prior to my visit, the water was covered with ice, and that he had to break out chunks of the ice and then wait for things to settle, just so they would have some open places to cast.

I looked down to see a strand of monofilament stuck to my wading boot. I reel it in on my hand and stuff it down into my jacket pocket. Later I feel rewarded for being a good steward as I snatch up a well-crafted green streamer fly that someone had dropped. Meanwhile, Cunningham is sight-casting to rainbows using a dropper rig. A fuzzy Stimulator rides high on the surface and a Beadhead Pheasant Tail Nymph drifts about four feet below. "Might as well have an indicator with a hook in it," he remarks. I asked him if he has a favorite fly? He said, "Anything yellow."

To get to Wilson Creek from Morganton, take N.C. 181 north to Brown Mountain Beach Road. Turn right and travel about 4.5 miles. After crossing Wilson Creek turn left (SR 1328), where Brown Mountain Beach Road turns north. Continue north and you will soon see Staac's store, a good place for fishing information. Continue through the Gorge Recreation Area and on to the Wilson Creek Visitor Center.

Types of Fish
Brook trout in the headwaters, predominantly rainbows elsewhere, and some browns.

Known Hatches
Baetis, Black Caddis, Black Stonefly, Blue Quill, Blue-Winged Olive, Cream Midge, Gray Caddis, Gray Fox, Green Drake, Hendrickson, Isonychia, Light Cahill, March Brown, midge, Quill Gordon, Giant Stonefly, terrestrials, Yellow Midge, Yellow Stonefly.

Equipment to Use
Rods: 3- to 4-weight for nymphs and dry flies, 5-weights for streamers, 6 to 8½ feet in length.
Reels: Any mechanical reel.
Lines: Floating lines to match rod weight.
Leaders: 9- to 12-foot leaders tapered to 4x through 6x.
Wading: Chest waders are recommended due to the deeper pools.

Flies to Use
Drys: Adams, sizes 16-18; Black Beetle, 14-16; Blue Thorax Dun, 18-22; Blue-Winged Olive Parachute, 14-20; Blue Quill, 14-18; Cahill, 14-20; Coffin Fly, 14-18; Dave's Hopper, 12-14; Elk-Hair Caddis, 16-18; Flying Ant, 12-18; Griffith's Glo Bug, 14-18; Gnat, 20; Gray Midge, 18-22; Hendrickson, 14-18; Humpy, 16-18; Inchworm, 14-18; Irresistible, 14-18; Little Yellow Sally, 14-20; March Brown, 16-18; Mosquito, 14-18; Quill Gordon, 12-20; Royal Coachman, 14-18; Royal Wulff, 14-18; Sheep Fly, 14-18; Stimulator, 12-18; Thunderhead, 12-16; Yellow Hammer, 10-14;

Nymphs & Streamers: Brassie, sizes 14-18; Beadhead Pheasant Tail Nymph, 16-18; Beadhead Gold-Ribbed Hare's Ear Nymph, 14-16; Bullethead Grasshopper, 10; Copper John, 14-18; Damsel, 14-16; Flashback Hare's Ear Nymph, 14-18; Gray Ghost, 8-12; Little Prince Nymph, 16-18; March Brown Nymph, 16-18; Mickey Finn, 8-10; Muddler Minnow, 6-10; Pat's Nymph; 18-24; San Juan Worm, 14-16; Scud, 12-18; Sculpin, 6-8; Stone Nymph, 6-10; Woolly Bugger, 6-10; Wickham's Nymph, 12-16.

When to Fish
Spring and fall are the ideal months.

Season & Limits
Wilson Creek is open to fishing all year long. The delayed-harvest section is marked by the game lands boundary (red bands on the trees) downstream of Lost Cove Creek to Phillips Branch just below Harper Creek. North and South Harper creeks are tributaries managed under the North Carolina Wildlife Resources Commission's Wild Trout regulations. Upper Wilson Creek is managed under the commission's Catch-and-Release, Artificial-Lures-Only regulations. Andrews Creek and Lost Cove Creek are also catch and release.

Nearby Fly Fishing
Catawba River, Linville Gorge.

Accommodations & Services
Brown Mountain Beach Resort has cabins and a store with some basic fly-fishing necessities. Mortimer Campground offers seasonal camping. Nearby Morganton offers a nice variety of lodging and shopping.

Helpful Web Sites
www.ncwildlife.org
www.brownmountainbeach.com

Rating
Wilson Creek, a National Wild and Scenic River, rates an 8.

Resources

This listing of resources is provided as a courtesy to help you enjoy your travels and fishing experience and is not intended to imply an endorsement of services either by the publisher or author. These listings are as accurate as possible as of the time of publication and are subject to change.

Asheville

Altamont Anglers
Asheville, NC 28803
(828) 775-0714
www.altamontanglers.com
guides

Brown Trout Fly Fishing
Inside the Orvis Store
28 Schenck Parkway,
Suite 150
Asheville, NC 28803
(803) 431-9437
www.browntroutflyfishing.com
guides

Curtis Wright Outfitters
5 All Souls Crescent
Asheville, NC 28803
(828) 274-3471
www.curtiswrightoutfitters.com
fly shop, guides, travel

Diamond Brand Outdoors
Downtown
53 Biltmore Avenue
Asheville, NC 28801
(828) 771-4761
www.diamondbrandoutdoors.com
outdoor store

Diamond Brand Outdoors
Parkway Center
1378 Hendersonville Road
Asheville, NC 28803
(828) 684-6262
www.diamondbrandoutdoors.com
outdoor store

Field & Stream
800 Brevard Road, Suite 901
Asheville, NC 28806
(828) 633-3182
www.fieldandstreamshop.com
fishing department

Fishwater River Guides
info@fishwaterguides.com
Asheville, NC
(828) 279-0959
www.fishwaterguides.com
guides

Hunter Banks Company
29 Montford Avenue
Asheville, NC 28801
(828) 252-3005
www.hunterbanks.com
fly shop, guides, instruction

Orvis
28 Schenck Parkway,
Suite 150
Asheville, NC 28803
(828) 678-0301
www.orvis.com
fly shop

Atlantic Beach

Cape Lookout Fly Shop
601-1 Atlantic Beach
Causeway
Atlantic Beach, NC 28512
(252) 240-1427
www.captjoes.com
fly shop, guides

Black Mountain

One Fly Outfitters
112 Cherry Street
Black Mountain, NC 28711
(828) 669-6939
www.oneflyoutfitters.com
fly shop, guides, instruction

Boone

Appalachian Angler
174 Old Shulls Mill Road
Boone, NC 28607
(828) 963-5050
www.appangler.com
fly shop, guides

Foscoe Fishing Company
8857 Highway 205 South
Boone, NC 28607
(828) 963-6556
www.foscoefishing.com
fly shop, guides

Brevard

Davidson River Outfitters
49 Pisgah Highway, Suite 6
Pisgah Forest, NC 28768
(828) 877-4181
www.davidsonflyfishing.com
fly shop, guides, instruction, travel

Bryson City

Fly Fishing Museum of the Southern Appalachians
210 Main Street
Bryson City, NC 28713
(828) 488-3681
www.flyfishingmuseum.org
museum

Nantahala Outdoor Center
13077 Highway 19 West
Bryson City, NC 28713
(828) 488-7230
www.noc.com
outdoor shop

Tuckaseegee Fly Shop
3 Depot Street
Bryson City, NC 28713
(828) 488-3333
www.tuckflyshop.com
fly shop, guides

Burnsville

Stonefly Outfitters
230 East Main Street
Burnsville, NC 28714
(828) 682-9233
www.stoneflyoutfittersnc.net
fly shop, guides

Cary

Bass Pro Shops
801 Bass Pro Lane
Cary, NC 27513
(919) 677-5100
www.basspro.com
White River fly shop

Cashiers

Brookings Anglers
49 Pillar Drive
Cashiers, NC 28717
(828) 743-3768
www.brookingsonline.com
fly shop, guides, lodging

Chapel Hill

Great Outdoor Provision Co.
1800 East Franklin Street
Eastgate Crossing
Chapel Hill, NC 27514
(919) 933-6148
www.greatoutdoorprovision.com
fishing department, instruction

Charlotte

Great Outdoor Provision Co.
4275 Park Road
Park Road Shopping Center
Charlotte, NC 28209
(704) 523-1089
www.greatoutdoorprovision.com
fishing department, instruction

Jesse Brown's Outdoors
4732 Sharon Road, Suite 2M
Charlotte, NC 28210
(704) 556-0020
www.jessebrowns.com
fly fishing department

Orvis
6800 Phillips Place Court,
Suite F
Charlotte, NC 28210
(704) 571-6100
www.orvis.com
fly shop

Cherokee

Rivers Edge Outfitters
61 Big Cove Road
Cherokee, NC 28719
(828) 497-9300
www.wncfishing.com
fly shop, guides, instruction, lodging

Concord

Academy Sports & Outdoors
8675 Concord Mills
Boulevard
Concord, NC 28027
(704) 808-4160
www.academy.com
fishing department

Bass Pro Shops
8181 Concord Mills
Boulevard
Concord, NC 28027
(704) 979-2200
www.basspro.com
White River fly shop

Cornelius

Madison River Fly Fishing Outfitters
20910 Torrence Chapel Road, Suite D5
Cornelius, NC 28031
(704) 896-3676
www.carolinaflyfishing.com
fly shop, guides, instruction, travel

Fayetteville

Academy Sports & Outdoors
2100 Skibo Road
Fayetteville, NC 28314
(910) 860-5100
www.academy.com
fishing department

Southern Outdoorsman
3011 Raeford Road
Fayetteville, NC 28303
(910) 433-0146
www.southernoutdoorsmannc.com
fly fishing department

Frisco

Frisco Rod & Gun
53610 Highway 12
Frisco, NC 27936
(252) 995-5366
www.friscorodandgun.com
outdoor shop

Garner

Cabela's
201 Cabela Drive
Garner, NC 27529
(984) 204-2200
www.cabelas.com
outdoor store

Greensboro

Academy Sports & Outdoors
4526 W. Wendover Avenue
Greensboro, NC 27409
(336) 632-3100
www.academy.com
fishing department

Field & Stream
1305 Bridford Parkway
Greensboro, NC 27407
(336) 419-1016
www.fieldandstreamshop.com
fishing department

Great Outdoor Provision Co.
3104 Northline Avenue
Friendly Shopping Center
Greensboro, NC 27408
(336) 851-1331
www.greatoutdoorprovision.com
fishing department, instruction

Orvis
Friendly Center
627 Friendly Center Road
Greensboro, NC 27408
(336) 547-7898
www.orvis.com
fly shop

Greenville

Academy Sports & Outdoors
3428 S. Memorial Drive
Greenville, NC 27834
(252) 329-2400
www.academy.com
fishing department

Great Outdoor Provision Co.
530-D SE Greenville
Boulevard
La Promenade II
Greenville, NC 27858
(252) 321-1308
www.greatoutdoorprovision.com
fishing department, instruction

Harker's Island

Harker's Island Fishing Center
1002 Island Road
Harker's Island, NC 28531
(252) 728-3907
www.harkersmarina.com
charters, instruction

Hickory

Academy Sports & Outdoors
2162 Highway 70 S.E.
Hickory, NC 28602
(828) 261-2550
www.academy.com
fishing department

Caster's Fly Shop
2427 N. Center Street
Hickory, NC 28601
(828) 304-2400
www.castersflyshop.com
fly shop, guides

Highlands

Brookings Anglers
273 Spring Street
Highlands, NC 28741
(828) 482-9444
www.brookingsonline.com
fly shop, guides, lodging

Highland Hiker
601 Main Street
Highlands, NC 28741
(828) 526-5298
www.highlandhiker.com
fly shop, guides

Jacksonville

Academy Sports & Outdoors
237 Samaria Drive
Jacksonville, NC 28546
(910) 937-3260
www.academy.com
fishing department

Kannapolis

Academy Sports & Outdoors
2211 Elder Lane
Kannapolis, NC 28083
(704) 260-4100
www.academy.com
fishing department

Kitty Hawk

Bob's Bait and Tackle
1180 Duck Road
Kitty Hawk, NC 27949
(252) 261-8589
www.bobsbaitandtackle.com
saltwater fishing, marine

TW's Bait & Tackle
3864 N. Croatan Highway
Kitty Hawk, NC 27949
(252) 261-7848
www.twstackle.com
saltwater fishing, marine

Linville

Highland Outfitters
4210 Mitchell Avenue #1
Linville, NC 28646
(828) 733-2181
www.highlandoutfittersnc.com
fly shop, guides

Marion

On the Fly Guide Service
Marion, NC 28752
(828) 659-0059
www.nconthefly.com
guides

Nags Head

Outer Banks Fly Fishing
Flat Out Charters
Fly Girl Charters
PO Box 387
Nag's Head, NC 27959
(252) 449-0562
www.outerbanksflyfishing.com
charters, instruction

TW's Bait & Tackle
2230 S. Croatan Highway
Nags Head, NC 27959
(252) 441-4807
www.twstackle.com
saltwater fishing, marine

Oriental

Spec Fever Guide Service
Capt. Gary Dubiel
100 Midyette Street
Oriental, NC 28571
(252) 249-1520
www.specfever.com
guides

Pisgah Forest

Davidson River Outfitters
49 Pisgah Highway, Suite 6
Pisgah Forest, NC 28768
(828) 877-4181
www.davidsonflyfishing.com
fly shop, guides, instruction, travel

Raleigh

Great Outdoor Provision Co.
2017 Cameron Street
Cameron Village
Raleigh, NC 27605
(919) 833-1741
www.greatoutdoorprovision.com
fishing department, instruction

Orvis
Triangle Town Commons
3701 Sumner Boulevard,
Suite 100
Raleigh, NC 27616
(919) 792-9200
www.orvis.com
fly shop

Rosman

Headwaters Outfitters
25 Parkway Road
Rosman, NC 28772
(828) 877-3106
www.headwatersoutfitters.com
fly shop, guides, paddling

Statesville

Carolina Mountain Sports
123 West Broad Street
Statesville, NC 28677
(704) 871-1444
www.carolinamountainsports.com
fly shop, outdoor store

Summerfield

Jeff Wilkins Fly Fishing
3703 Windspray Court
Summerfield, NC 27358
(336) 944-3628
www.appflyguide.com
guide

Sylva

Black Rock Outdoor Company/Orvis Fly Shop
570 West Main Street
Sylva, NC 28779
(828) 631-4453
www.blackrockoutdoor
company.com
fly shop, guides, rentals

Hookers Fly Shop
546 West Main Street
Sylva, NC 28779
(828) 587-4665
www.hookersflyshop.com
fly shop, guides

Tuckaseegee Fly Shop
530 West Main Street
Sylva, NC 28779
(828) 488-3333
www.tuckflyshop.com
fly shop, guides

Todd

RiverGirl Fishing Co.
4041 Todd Railroad Grade
Road
Todd, NC 28684
(336) 877-3099
www.rivergirlfishing.com
fly shop, guides, instruction

Waynesville

Hunter Banks Company
48 North Main Street
Waynesville, NC 28786
(828) 251-9721
www.hunterbanks.com
fly shop, guides, instruction

Weaverville

Curtis Wright Outfitters
24 North Main Street
Weaverville, NC 28787
(828) 645-8700
www.curtiswrightoutfitters.com
fly shop, guides, travel

Wilmington

Great Outdoor Provision Co.
3501 Oleander Drive
(US 76)
Hanover Center
Wilmington, NC 28403
(910) 343-1648
www.greatoutdoorprovision.com
fishing department, instruction

Hook, Line, & Paddle
435 Eastwood Road
Wilmington, NC 28403
(910) 792-6945
www.hooklineandpaddle.com
kayak fishing guide

Intracoastal Angler
6332 Oleander Drive
Wilmington, NC 28403
(910) 392-3500
www.intracoastalangler.com
fly shop, saltwater guides

Sightfish NC
Wilmington, NC
(336) 613-2975
www.sightfishnc.com
guide

Winston-Salem

Blue Ridge Custom Flies
www.blueridgecustomflies.com
flies, custom flies

Great Outdoor Provision Co.
402 S. Stratford Road
Thruway Shopping Center
Winston-Salem, NC 27103
(336) 727-0906
www.greatoutdoorprovision.com
fishing department, instruction

The Green Drake
123 S. Stratford Road
Winston-Salem, NC 27104
(336) 723-9070
www.thegreendrake.com
fly shop, instruction, travel

Wrightsville Beach

Reel Adventure Charters
Capt. Matt Wirt
(910) 540-0570
www.reel-adventure.com
saltwater guides

ORGANIZATIONS

Fly Fishers International (FFI)
7 Groups in North Carolina
www.flyfishersinternational.org

Project Healing Waters Fly Fishing
10 Programs throughout
North Carolina
(301) 830-6450
www.projecthealingwaters.org

Trout Unlimited
16 Chapters throughout
North Carolina
www.tu.org

Conservation

No Nonsense Fly Fishing Guidebooks believes that, in addition to local information and gear, fly fishers need clean water and healthy fish. We encourage preservation, improvement, conservation, enjoyment, and understanding of our waters and their inhabitants. While fly fishing, take care of the place, practice catch and release, and try to avoid spawning fish.

When you aren't fly fishing, a good way to help all things wild and aquatic is to support organizations dedicated to these ideas. We encourage you to get involved, learn more, and to join such organizations.

American Conservation Experience (ACE)..(928) 226-6960
American Rivers...(202) 347-7550
Blackfoot Challenge..(406) 793-9300
California Trout...(415) 392-8887
Camo Coalition...(770) 787-7887
Cape Fear River Watch...(910) 762-5606
Catawba River Keeper Foundation..(704) 679-9494
Chattahoochee Coldwater Fishery Foundation..(770) 650-8630
Chesapeake Bay Foundation...(410) 268-8816
Coastal Conservation Association Virginia...(804) 966-5654
Deschutes Basin Land Trust..(541) 330-0017
Fly Fishers International...(406) 222-9369
Georgia Department of Natural Resources (Fisheries)................................(770) 918-6406
Georgia Outdoor Network...(800) 866-5516
International Game Fish Association..(954) 927-2628
International Women Fly Fishers..(925) 934-2461
New Mexico Trout...(505) 884-5262
North Carolina Wildlife Federation (NCWF)..(919) 833-1923
North Carolina Youth Conservation Corps (NCYCC).................................(919) 828-4199
Oregon Trout..(503) 222-9091
Outdoor Writers Association of America...(406) 728-7434
Recreational Fishing Alliance...(888) 564-6732
Rails-to-Trails Conservancy...(202) 331-9696
Theodore Roosevelt Conservation Partnership...(877) 770-8722
Trout Unlimited...(800) 834-2419

Find Your Way with These No Nonsense Guides

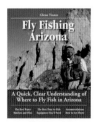

Fly Fishing Arizona
ISBN 978-1-892469-02-1
$18.95

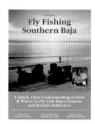

**Fly Fishing
Southern Baja**
ISBN 978-1-892469-00-7
$18.95

Fly Fishing California
ISBN 978-1-892469-10-6
$28.95

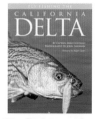

**Fly Fishing the
California Delta**
ISBN 978-1-892469-23-6
$49.95

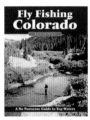

Fly Fishing Colorado
ISBN 978-1-892469-13-7
$19.95

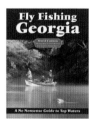

Fly Fishing Georgia
ISBN 978-1-892469-20-5
$28.95

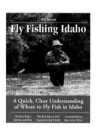

Fly Fishing Idaho
ISBN 978-1-892469-17-5
$18.95

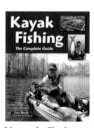

**Kayak Fishing
2nd Edition**
ISBN 978-1-892469-25-0
$24.95

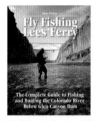

Fly Fishing Lees Ferry
ISBN 978-1-892469-15-1
$18.95

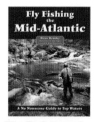

**Fly Fishing the
Mid-Atlantic**
ISBN 978-1-892469-24-3
$29.95

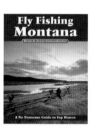

Fly Fishing Montana
ISBN 978-1-892469-14-4
$28.95

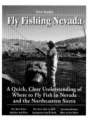

Fly Fishing Nevada
ISBN 978-0-9637256-2-2
$18.95

Fly Fishing New Mexico
ISBN 978-1-892469-04-5
$18.95

**Fly Fishing Central &
Southeastern Oregon**
ISBN 978-1-892469-09-0
$19.95

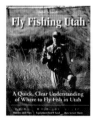

Fly Fishing Utah
ISBN 978-0-9637256-8-4
$19.95

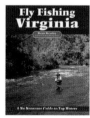

Fly Fishing Virginia
ISBN 978-1-892469-16-8
$28.95

Business Traveler's Guide To Fly Fishing in the Western States • ISBN 978-1-892469-01-4 • $18.95

Fishing Central California • ISBN 978-1-892469-18-2 • $24.95

Fly Fishing Pyramid Lake • ISBN 978-0-9637256-3-9 • $15.95

Seasons of the Metolius • ISBN 978-1-892469-11-3 • $20.95

Fly Fishing Magdalena Bay • ISBN 978-1-892469-08-3 • $24.95

Fly-Fishing Knots

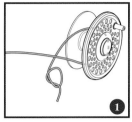 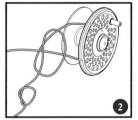 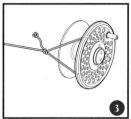

Arbor Knot: *(Above) Use this knot to attach backing to your fly reel.*

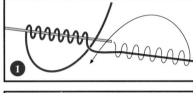

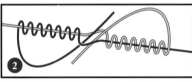

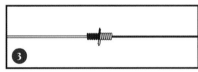

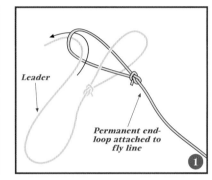

Leader

Permanent end-loop attached to fly line

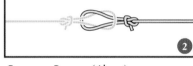

Blood Knot: *(Above)*
Use this knot to connect sections of leader tippet material. Hard to tie, but worth the effort.

Loop-to-Loop: *(Above)*
Easy connection of leader to a permanent monofilament end loop added to the tip of the fly line.

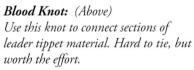

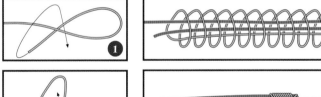

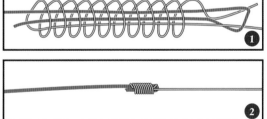

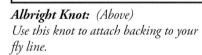

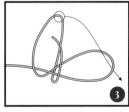

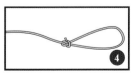

Albright Knot: *(Above)*
Use this knot to attach backing to your fly line.

Perfection Loop: *(Left)*
Use this knot to create a loop in the butt end of the leader for loop-to-loop connections.

Nail Knot: *(Right)*
Use a nail, needle or a tube to tie this knot, which connects the forward end of the fly line to the butt end of the leader. Follow with a Perfection Loop and you've got a permanent end loop that allows easy leader changes.

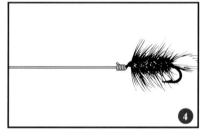

Improved Clinch Knot: *(Above)*
Use this knot to attach the fly to the end of the tippet. Remember to moisten the knot before pulling it up tight.

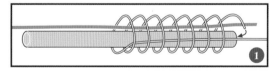

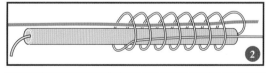

Fly Line

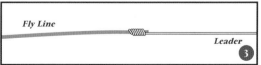

Leader

Autumn is a spectacular time in the North Carolina mountains, especially if you are an angler in the Nantahala Gorge.